UNDERSTANDING

LD*

*LEARNING DIFFERENCES

UNDERSTANDING

LD*

*LEARNING DIFFERENCES

A Curriculum to Promote
LD Awareness, Self-Esteem
and Coping Skills in
Students Ages 8-13

BY SUSAN McMURCHIE, M.A.

EDITED BY PAMELA ESPELAND

*Free
Spirit* ®
PUBLISHING

10 9 8 7 6 5 4 3 2 1

Printed in the United States of America

Cover and book design by MacLean & Tuminelly

Index compiled by Eileen Quam and Theresa Wolner

The following handouts have been adapted or reprinted from *The Survival Guide for Kids with LD (Learning Differences)* by Gary Fisher, Ph.D., and Rhoda Cummings, Ed.D. (Free Spirit Publishing, 1990) with permission of the publisher: "Teasing Response Rating" (page 47) and "10 Tips for Making and Keeping Friends" (page 67). The following handouts have been adapted or reprinted from *The School Survival Guide for Kids with LD (Learning Differences)* by Rhoda Cummings, Ed.D., and Gary Fisher, Ph.D. (Free Spirit Publishing, 1991) with permission of the publisher: "My Routine" (page 105), "Time Chart" (page 106), "Things to Do" (page 110), "Draw Between the Lines" (page 115), and "Crossword Puzzle Form" (page 116).

Free Spirit Publishing Inc.
400 First Avenue North, Suite 616
Minneapolis, MN 55401-1730
(612) 338-2068

Dedication

To my husband, Tom, and my daughter, Ryan, for all of their
encouragement and support.

To all of the wonderful students I have worked with.
Your courage and cooperation have been remarkable!

Acknowledgments

Thanks to Deb Gillman, my Master's Degree advisor, who introduced me
to curriculum design and who encouraged me to use it in an affective domain.

Thanks also to the Saint Mary's College of Minnesota faculty, who stress
practical application of learned concepts.

Finally, thanks to Pamela Espeland, my editor, and Judy Galbraith, my publisher,
for believing in proactive ways to help children with learning differences.

Contents

List of Reproducible Pages

Introduction

During the course of teaching elementary school students with learning disabilities, it became apparent to me that many of them had no idea of why they were working with me, other than that they needed extra help. When asked, "What is a learning disability?," the majority couldn't answer. When asked, "Has anyone ever told you that you have learning disabilities?," almost all of them responded, "No." Some of them may have been told by their parents or teachers, but they didn't remember.

As these students were preparing to go to middle school, I was expecting that they would be able to advocate for themselves—to articulate their needs, talk about their problems, stand up to teasing, and make friends on their own terms. But this was not happening. Even more discouraging, I began to notice that many of my fourth and fifth graders were expressing negative feelings about themselves and their capabilities. I realized that all of my remedial work with them would be in vain if I did not help these children become more aware of their learning disabilities and more accepting of themselves. It was then that I created "The Lunch Bunch," a special group for my students with LD that met during the lunch period twice a month.

My objective was to provide a safe, relaxed setting where my students could build LD awareness, develop strategies for coping, share their difficulties, help each other, learn together, and most of all have fun getting to know each other better. Meanwhile, I discovered two books that would become very important to my students and to me:

- *The Survival Guide for Kids with LD (Learning Differences)* by Gary Fisher, Ph.D., and Rhoda Cummings, Ed.D. (Free Spirit Publishing, 1990) is the first Survival Guide for children labeled "learning disabled." It explains LD in terms kids can understand, describes the different kinds of LD, discusses LD programs, and emphasizes that kids with LD can be winners, too.

- *The School Survival Guide for Kids with LD (Learning Differences): Ways to Make Learning Easier and More Fun* by Rhoda Cummings, Ed.D., and Gary Fisher, Ph.D. (Free Spirit Publishing, 1991) presents specific tips and strategies for making school easier and more fun.

These two books and my Lunch Bunch were a natural match. While pursuing my master's degree, I developed a formal curriculum based on the Survival Guides, and this became the predecessor of *Understanding LD*.

The goal of this curriculum is to create an awareness of learning disabilities, which I now call "learning differences" because that term is more positive and affirming and also is closer to the truth: all students learn differently, each in his or her own way. The lessons and activities help students to focus on their similarities and differences and to begin developing coping strategies for school and social situations. They give students opportunities to become more accepting of themselves and aware of how they learn, and, ultimately, to develop a positive self-concept and self-advocacy skills.

This curriculum was originally designed for fourth and fifth graders, with two 60-minute sessions per month from October through May. It has also been used effectively with a mixed group of fifth through seventh graders meeting once a month for 90-minute sessions, and with fourth graders meeting once a month. Since the Survival Guides upon which this curriculum is based were written for grades three and up, you may find that you are able to use it with third graders as well.

1

It's easy to customize the curriculum and the individual sessions to meet the needs of your students. For me, every year is different.

Understanding LD is divided into several sections that emphasize important topics for students with LD. The essential sessions are found in Part One: LD Awareness. These six sessions are the foundation for the curriculum, the base of knowledge and understanding that all the other sessions should build on. You may pick and choose from among the remaining sessions, depending on how much time you have and what you want to accomplish with your group. The curriculum also has been designed to allow you to incorporate other materials—books, audios, filmstrips, videos—as available and as appropriate for your students. Any of the topics can be extended over more than one session.

Just as I developed this curriculum originally to meet the needs of my students, I encourage you to adapt it to meet the needs of yours.

Forming Your Group

Any students you invite to your group must already have been identified as LD. This is imperative! The permission letter that parents receive from you (see page 6) should *not* be the first time they hear that their child has a learning difference. There are laws and assessment procedures which must be followed to correctly identify children with LD. If you have any questions, check with your district.

How large should your group be? In my experience, group size depends on my caseload and the number of students with LD at each grade level. Sometimes I conduct a group with another LD teacher and the students on his or her caseload. Groups need to be large enough to allow for a variety of responses, but if they are too large, some children are less likely to participate. My best groups have had from six to twelve students. It's good to have both boys and girls in the group, although it may not always be possible. Because the number of boys who have been identified as LD is so much larger than the number of girls, there may be times when your group has very few girls. You'll need to be especially sensitive to their feelings.

It's important to talk with the students in advance—individually or in small groups—about your desire to have them be part of the group. Briefly explain what will happen during the sessions, and let them know who else may be coming to the group. Tell them that the group will give them a chance to feel better about their learning differences, to get to know other students who are in exactly the same situation they are in, and especially to have fun. Explain that you will have to get their parents' permission before they can come to the group, and tell them that their participation is optional but you hope very much that they will decide to join.

It's a good idea to let parents know about the group before sending out the permission letter, perhaps at a special education staffing or conference. Encourage parents to talk about the group with their children.

At times, I have had each student sign a contract promising to follow the rules of the group (see page 7) and pledging that they want to improve their lives and are willing to try some things they learn in group in their classrooms and at home. If a student has problems along the way with attitude or behavior, a reminder of the contract is usually enough to get the student back on track. If a student expresses negative feelings about being in the group, either before or after it starts, I arrange a private meeting so I can hear and acknowledge his or her feelings. I encourage the student to commit to at least two or three sessions before making the decision to drop out. I also talk to the parents to find out if there's anything more about the student I need to know, and also to encourage the parents to talk to their child about staying in the group. I never force a student to join the group or to remain in the group if he or she truly wants to leave.

Getting Ready

Before your first group meeting, familiarize yourself with the session focuses and procedures. Decide which sessions you will be presenting and assemble the materials you will need; these are listed at the beginning of each session. Read over the supplemental sessions (pages 117–126) and the Children's Literature section (pages 127–142). Decide which, if any, books you will want to include in the sessions. You'll notice that each title listed includes complete bibliographical information, and several also include discussion questions. The book I use most often (and, as a result, have provided the most discussion questions for) is *Josh: A Boy with Dyslexia.*

Because this curriculum is based on *The Survival Guide for Kids with LD* and *The School Survival Guide for Kids with LD,* I highly recommend that multiple copies of both books (and of the audio cassette for the first *Survival Guide*) be available for use during the sessions. Your students can check them out between sessions. Ideally, each student in the group will have his or her own copies of both books. Free Spirit Publishing offers discounts for quantity purchases; for more information, call toll-free 1-800-735-7323.

Try to find a private place to hold your meetings. Students will be more willing to share if they feel that they will not be seen or heard by others who are not in the group. The room should be flexible enough to allow for individual work, small group work, and large group discussions. For most sessions, you may want to arrange chairs, desks, or tables in a circle.

Since this curriculum includes several handouts, I strongly recommend that you give each student a folder (or three-ring binder) for collecting and storing materials used and created in the group. Distribute the folders during the first session, and remind the students to bring their folders to every group meeting. Keep extra copies of handouts available for times when students forget to bring their folders. Or, depending on your group, you might want to collect the folders at the end of each session and store them in a box or on a shelf between sessions. At the end of the group experience, each student will have a useful and informative collection of materials for future reference and to share with his or her parents.

There are some handouts you may want to send home to parents immediately after a session. You'll need to make extra copies of these as well.

There is one supplemental session which formally addresses "success stories" (session 21, pages 119–120). However, it is very important that the idea of student success be woven into the curriculum as much as possible. This can easily be done at various points during the sessions. The Children's Literature section lists and describes several relevant books you may want to have on hand and turn to whenever it seems appropriate. Discussion questions are included for each title.

Communicating with Parents

You'll need to get parental permission for each student to participate in your group. On page 6, you'll find a permission letter to photocopy, fill out, and send home with students. Or use this as a starting point for creating your own permission letter.

It's important to establish and maintain good communication with parents. Make yourself available to parents who want to meet with you and discuss what the group will be doing. Be ready to explain why you believe their son or daughter is a good candidate for your group, and emphasize how participation will benefit the child. Be prepared to answer questions from parents who want to know more about the group and who may be concerned that their child has been "singled out."

Throughout the year (or for however long your group continues to meet), send home copies of interesting handouts, notes to parents, and occasionally a brief newsletter describing the group's activities and progress. Most parents like to be informed of what their children are doing in school. The more informed they are, the more likely they will be to support your efforts and reinforce what their children are learning in your group.

Actually, it's a good idea to send brief notes home to parents after *each* session. Whenever I have done this, it has proved to be an excellent way to keep in touch and elicit parents' support. My notes usually include descriptions about what the group has been doing, definitions of key words and concepts, and a special "Things for You to Reinforce" section with specific suggestions for how parents can follow up at home. I always end my notes by thanking parents for their support and cooperation.

Communicating with Classroom Teachers

You'll also want to establish and maintain contact with the regular classroom teachers (or "mainstream teachers") of the children in your group. Start with a general informational meeting before the group begins. Tell the teachers what your group will be doing and how this will help

their students with LD to get along better in the regular classroom. (Naturally, this will make their jobs easier; be sure to mention this!) Some teachers will want to see the curriculum in advance. Let them, and invite their comments and questions. You may want to schedule monthly meetings to keep teachers informed of the group's activities and progress. The more teachers know, the more they will be able to support and reinforce your efforts.

Teachers, like parents, appreciate notes and newsletters. I usually include brief summary statements of concepts and skills covered in our meetings, plus "Things for You to Reinforce" suggestions for follow-up in the regular classroom.

When I first presented this curriculum, I was able to do it during lunch time and not disrupt regular classroom schedules. This may be possible for you, or it may not. If you must present *Understanding LD* as a pull-out program because of schedule conflicts or other reasons, you'll need to make an extra effort to win the support of the classroom teachers.

Eight Tips for Leading Great Groups

1. Establish the Group Rules immediately and reinforce them often (see page 14). Post the rules in the meeting room and make a copy for each student. Discuss the rules with the students to make sure that everyone understands what they mean.

2. Make sure that the students understand your role as group leader. Explain that although they will have many opportunities to talk and listen to each other, you'll be keeping the group on task and aware of the session focus.

3. Be aware of your time frame for each session. While you want to give all children the chance to contribute, you need to keep the session moving. Try to allow enough time to end the session without rushing.

4. Establish group confidentiality. It's critically important for students to know that anything they say in the group stays in the group (this is Group Rule #5—it's worth extra emphasis). Tell them that this applies to everyone, including you.

5. Encourage students to participate, but don't insist. Not volunteering is okay. It takes some students longer than others to start contributing. Meanwhile, they need to feel that it's fine just to sit quietly and observe.

6. Tell the students that the more they work together, accept one another, and share their good ideas, the more fun they will have.

7. Let them know that the group is a safe place for them to be. Tell them that they are accepted here for who they are, just as they are, with no pressure to perform.

8. Although group participation should never be graded, you may want a way to keep track of how your students are doing. On page 8, you'll find a Student Assessment Form that has been specially designed for this purpose. Start one for each student in your group, and do your record-keeping as soon as possible after each session. You will probably find these forms to be very helpful in consultations with individual students, their parents, and their teachers.

OPTIONAL: Consider asking students to sign a contract at the beginning of the group. On page 7, you'll find a Student Contract that I have used successfully in my groups.

Your Child Is Invited...

Dear Parent(s),

Your son or daughter has been invited to join a discussion group at school. The group is especially for students with LD. While LD means "learning disabilities" to some people, in our group it means "learning differences," because all students learn in their own unique ways.

The group will help students to become more aware of their learning differences, to develop coping strategies, and to see themselves as capable, competent people. Many students with learning differences have a negative self-concept and low self-esteem. Some have grown accustomed to failure and problems in school. They may even think that they are "stupid" or "dumb." In our group, they will learn that they are definitely not "stupid" or "dumb." They just learn differently.

The group will be a safe place for students to get to know each other and themselves. There will be no pressure to "perform." The lessons and activities will promote self-awareness and positive self-esteem. I believe that this group will benefit your child, and that you will soon notice some positive changes at home.

The group will begin on _____. I need your permission for your child to participate. Please complete the bottom part of this form and return it to me by _____. If you have any questions about the group, feel free to call me at _____.

Sincerely,

- -

My child, _____,
              (Name of child)

____ has my permission to participate in the discussion group.

____ does not have my permission to participate in the discussion group.

_____   _____
(Parent signature)   (Date)

Student Contract

I understand that this group is a time to have fun. I understand that this group is also a time to:

▶ learn ways to understand my learning differences,

▶ learn ways to understand myself better, and

▶ learn ways to make positive changes in my life.

I promise to follow the group rules.

I promise to try the things I learn in this group.
I will try them at home and in my classroom.

When I am in this group, it is my responsibility to cooperate.

I agree to be accepting of everyone else in this group.

Signed: _____

Date: _____

Student Assessment Form

Name of student: _____

Date	On Task	Participation	Attitude	Comments

PART

LD Awareness

I Am, I Can

LD Awareness Focus

Students formulate one question about learning differences they would like to have answered before the group ends. They write one thing about their learning difference(s) that bothers them.

Self-Esteem Focus

Students listen to the story, "I Am, I Can," and prepare their own "I Am, I Can" sign to use when sharing the story with their parents.

Materials Needed

Handouts

- "Welcome" (page 13)
- "Group Rules" (page 14)
- "'I Am, I Can' List" (page 15)
- "I Am, I Can" story (page 17)
- "Five Facts about 'I Am, I Can'" (pages 18–19)

Supplies

- Paper, pencils, and markers, enough for all students

- Folders, one for each student (write their names on the folders ahead of time)

- Tape

- One copy of the "I Am, I Can" sign (page 16) for use during the story

- *The Survival Guide for Kids with LD*

- **Optional:** *The Survival Guide for Kids with LD* audio cassette

- **Optional:** *Josh: A Boy with Dyslexia* or any other book of your choice from the Children's Literature section (pages 127–142)

The Session

1. Welcome the students. Introduce the children to each other, or have them introduce themselves.

2. Distribute the "Welcome" handout. Read it aloud and use it to explain the purpose of the group. Say, "During our meetings, we will be supporting each other, learning together, and building friendships."

3. Distribute the "Group Rules" handout. Go over the rules one at a time. Make sure that the students understand the rules.

4. Read aloud the Introduction to *The Survival Guide for Kids with LD* (pages 1–6) or play the audio cassette. Then ask, "Who can tell me what LD means?" Answers might include "Learning Disabled," "Learning Disabilities," or "Learning Different" (the meaning given in the book). Some students might answer "dumb," "retarded," "mental," "stupid," "lazy," etc.

Listen to all responses. Then say, "In this group, LD *always* means 'learning different' or 'learning differences.' Everybody learns in their own way. Everybody learns differently. Some people are good at some things and not good at other things. LD *never* means 'dumb,' 'retarded,' [or other negative words students used]. We will not use those words in this group."

5. Distribute paper and pencils. Say, "Fold your paper in half. Write your name on the top. Then open your paper. On one half, write one question you have about LD that you would like an answer for. On the other half, write one gripe you have about your own LD. If you want, you can write more than one question and gripe."

Collect the papers for use in Session 2. Make copies for your files so you are sure to have the questions and the gripes for future reference.

6. Distribute the "'I Am, I Can' List" handout. Read through the statements and invite students to complete the last three. Say, "These are very important statements we all must practice using. I'm going to share a story with you that will show you why we need to be able to use these statements."

7. Show the group the "I Am, I Can" sign. Then read aloud the "I Am, I Can" story (page 17). As you read, rip and tape the sign at the appropriate times.

8. Distribute paper, markers, and copies of the "I Am, I Can" story. Invite the students to make their own "I Am, I Can" signs to take home. Encourage them to share the story with their parents.

9. Distribute the "Five Facts about 'I Am, I Can'" handout. Read through the statements. Emphasize their importance. Say, "During the next session, we will be learning specific ways to take care of our own 'I Am, I Can' signs."

10. Distribute the folders. Point out that each group member has his or her own folder. Say, "We will be using these to collect the handouts and other materials we use in this group."

Instruct the students to put the handouts from this session in their folders. They will be taking the stories home, so you may want to have extra copies of the stories for their folders.

11. **Optional:** Introduce the book, *Josh: A Boy with Dyslexia,* and read aloud Chapter 1 (pages 1–6). Or introduce and read from an alternate title from the Children's Literature section. Allow time for questions and discussion.

12. End the session by thanking the students for coming and for sharing with each other. Tell them to be sure to take care of their "I Am, I Can" signs between now and the next session. Remind them to bring their folders to the next session.

SESSION 1

Welcome!

This group is for students who have been told they have a learning disability and who may not be sure just what that means.

You may be having trouble with some of your school work. Some people think that having trouble in school means that you are dumb. THAT IS NOT TRUE! If you were dumb, you would have trouble learning and doing everything. But you only have trouble learning and doing some things. And you can learn and do those things with practice and help.

In this group, you will find out what it means to have learning disabilities. But we don't call them learning disabilities. We call them learning differences. Everybody learns differently, not just people with LD.

Once you understand better what it means to have learning differences, you will understand yourself more. You will like yourself more.

Share what you learn with your parents. Sometimes they have trouble understanding LD.

Remember:
The problems you have aren't the most important thing.
What you do about your problems is the most important thing.

SESSION 1

Group Rules

1

Only one person talks at a time.

2

When someone is talking, everyone else listens.

3

It's okay not to talk if you don't feel like talking.

4

We make positive, constructive comments about each other.
No criticism or making fun.

5

Everything we say in the group stays in the group.

SESSION 1

"I Am, I Can" List

I am special.

I'm worth it.

I deserve this.

I can do it.

I can handle this.

I'm worth being friends with.

I can cope.

I will make it through this.

I can keep trying.

I can stick with it.

I will try my best.

I am really good at _____.

I did a nice job on _____.

I was helpful when I _____.

SESSION 1

I AM,
I CAN

SESSION 1

I Am, I Can

This is a story about a boy I am going to call Johnny. However, the name is not important. It could be Maria, Ann, Jake, Sam, or anyone.

It is 7:00 in the morning and the alarm goes off. Johnny is starting his day. The first thing he does is to put on his "I Am, I Can" sign.

Johnny decides to crawl back into bed just for a few minutes. Suddenly, he is awakened by his mother's yelling, "Get out of bed this very minute, you lazy thing!" This RIPS off a piece of his "I Am, I Can" sign.

Johnny's sister calls him a little creep when he tells her to hurry up and get out of the bathroom because he is running late. Another piece of his "I Am, I Can" sign is RIPPED off.

After breakfast, Johnny's mother apologizes for calling him lazy. She gives him a kiss and a hug and tells him to have a good day. This PUTS A PIECE BACK on his "I Am, I Can" sign.

As Johnny boards the bus to school, he notices his friends sitting together at the back. They pretend not to see him and don't ask him to join them. Another piece of Johnny's "I Am, I Can" sign is RIPPED off.

When Johnny arrives at school, he realizes that he left his math homework at home. In math class, his teacher is angry with him for forgetting it. What happens to his "I Am, I Can" sign?

In gym class, Johnny is the last person picked to be on the volleyball team. What happens to his "I Am, I Can" sign?

In language class, Johnny gets seven wrong on his practice spelling test. He is very mad at himself because he didn't get more right. What does he do to his own "I Am, I Can" sign?

As the day goes on, good and bad things continue to happen in Johnny's life. When he goes to bed that night, he takes his "I Am, I Can" sign off. It is much smaller than it was in the morning.

SESSION 1

Five Facts about "I Am, I Can"

1

Your "I Am, I Can" sign needs TLC (Tender Loving Care) EVERY day.

2

These are some things that can harm your "I Am, I Can" sign:

▶ mean criticism (from others or from yourself)

▶ being judged unfairly

▶ teasing

▶ being ignored or left out

3

A rip in your "I Am, I Can" sign is SERIOUS! You need immediate Self-Esteem First Aid. If you can't get it from another person, you'll have to give it to yourself. Tell yourself "I Am Smart, I Can Do It!" Or choose a saying from your "'I Am, I Can' List" to tell yourself.

Five Facts about "I Am, I Can" continued

4

These are some things that can keep your "I Am, I Can" sign healthy and whole:

- ▶ kindness
- ▶ someone who listens to you
- ▶ encouragement (from others or from yourself)
- ▶ being appreciated
- ▶ forgiveness (by others or by yourself)
- ▶ understanding

5

You are responsible for taking care of your own "I Am, I Can" sign. You are also responsible for not harming anyone else's "I Am, I Can" sign.

Remember:

Other people want to be treated the same way YOU want to be treated.

Session 1

Affirmations

LD Awareness Focus

Students formulate answers to their own questions about learning differences.

Self-Esteem Focus

Students give positive affirmations to themselves and one another.

Materials Needed

Handouts

- "'I Am, I Can' Journal" (page 23), enough for each student to last for one to two weeks

- Extra copies of the "'I Am, I Can' List" (Session 1, page 15)

Supplies

- Poster paper, pencils, and markers, enough for all students

- Whiteboard, chalkboard, or flip chart; marker or chalk

- Students' questions and gripes saved from Session 1

- A list of positive words or phrases beginning with the letters of the students' names (see #12 in "The Session")

- *The Survival Guide for Kids with LD*

- **Optional:** *The Survival Guide for Kids with LD* audio cassette

- **Optional:** *Josh: A Boy with Dyslexia* or any other book of your choice from the Children's Literature section (pages 127–142)

The Session

1. Welcome the students back to the group and allow a few moments for conversation. Say, "Today you will find out some answers to the questions about LD you wrote during the last session. You will also have the chance to share your gripes. Plus we'll learn how to fix rips in your 'I Am, I Can' sign."

2. Distribute the students' questions and gripes from Session 1. Invite the students to share their questions. Write them on the board or flip chart.

3. Read aloud "Ten More Things You Might Want to Know about LD" from *The Survival Guide for Kids with LD* (pages 77–82) or play the audio cassette. Afterward, draw the group's attention to the questions you wrote on the board or flip chart. For each question, ask, "How would you answer this question?" Record responses.

Leave blank any questions students can't answer immediately. Return to these when the remaining questions have been answered and ask, "Does anyone have ideas for these now?" Have the students work together in pairs or small groups to come up with possible answers. Record them on the board or flip chart.

4. Invite the students to share their gripes. Record them on the board or flip chart. Ask, "Do you agree that these are problems for kids with learning differences?" Ask if anyone has a new gripe to add to the list.

5. Ask, "Can someone tell me what a compliment is?" Give examples by complimenting each student in the group. Then ask, "How does it feel to get a compliment?"

6. Invite the students to compliment one another. Then ask, "How does it feel to give a compliment?"

7. Ask, "Have you ever given yourself a compliment?" Give examples of compliments students might give themselves: "I did a good job on that assignment," "I knew I could read this story. It was hard, but I tried my best," "I'm good at making friends," "I'm a really fast runner," "I have a nice smile," etc.

Invite the students to compliment themselves. Then ask, "How does it feel to give yourself a compliment?"

8. Say, "Another word for a compliment is 'affirmation.' Giving and getting affirmations makes us feel good. It also feels good to give ourselves affirmations. This is something we can do for ourselves every day."

Ask, "What would an affirmation—from someone else, or from you to yourself—do to a rip in your 'I Am, I Can' sign?"

9. Ask students to take the "'I Am, I Can' List" out of their folders. (Distribute extra copies to students who need them.) Read through the statements and say, "These are all affirmations we can give ourselves."

Distribute pencils and encourage the students to add more affirmations to the list. Invite them to share their new affirmations.

10. Say, "There are other kinds of affirmations besides words. A kind action—helping another person, doing something nice just because, or smiling at someone—can also be an affirmation. Positive words and actions are both very powerful." Ask the students to give examples of affirming actions and behaviors.

11. Distribute the "'I Am, I Can' Journal" handout. Have the children complete one day. Model this for them on the board or flip chart. Explain that they can use their "'I Am, I Can' List" for ideas. Tell them to write in their journals every day, even on days when the group doesn't meet.

NOTE: This activity can be difficult for some children because they are not used to focusing on the positive things about themselves. They may

21

need a great deal of modeling and encouragement to get in the habit of keeping their journals. However, if used consistently, the journals can become a powerful tool for helping them feel good about themselves.

12. Distribute poster paper and markers. Say, "We are going to make positive affirmation name posters. Start by printing your name in large letters along the left side of your paper. Then pick one letter and write a positive word or phrase about yourself that starts with that letter."

Model this on the board or flip chart. Use your own name or the name of a student in your group. Example: "G-R-E-G. G is for Great. R is for Responsible. E is for Excellent. G is for Good Swimmer."

Say, "After you do one letter, pass your paper to another student. Then write a positive word or phrase about the person whose paper you have." (If the group is sitting in a circle, you might instruct them to pass to the right or the left.)

Make sure that everyone understands what they will be doing. Allow time for students to complete the posters. Explain that it's okay to write more than one word or phrase for students with shorter names. Be ready to help with the list of adjectives you prepared in advance.

The posters can be sent home with the students or collected and displayed during future sessions.

13. **Optional:** Read aloud Chapters 2 and 3 of *Josh: A Boy with Dyslexia* (pages 7–15). Or read from an alternate title from the Children's Literature section. Allow time for questions and discussion.

14. End the session by reminding the students to fill out their journals every day. Say, "Remember, this is a great way to take care of your 'I Am, I Can' signs." Remind them to bring their folders to the next session.

SESSION 2

"I Am, I Can" Journal

by _____

Date	Affirmation to myself	Affirmation from someone else

How LD Affects Me

LD Awareness Focus

Students learn about ways their LD can affect them, and they assess their own strengths and weaknesses.

Self-Esteem Focus

Students learn that they have peers who are like them and who accept them for who they are.

Materials Needed

Handouts

- "What Are Learning Differences?" (pages 26–28)
- "How LD Affects Me" (pages 29–30)
- Extra copies of the "'I Am, I Can' Journal" (Session 2, page 23)

Supplies

- Pencils, enough for all students
- Whiteboard, chalkboard, or flip chart; marker or chalk
- *The Survival Guide for Kids with LD*
- **Optional:** *The Survival Guide for Kids with LD* audio cassette
- **Optional:** *Josh: A Boy with Dyslexia* or any other book of your choice from the Children's Literature section (pages 127–142)

The Session

1. Welcome the students and give them time to talk about how their days have been going. Reinforce the positive things that have been happening to them.

Ask, "Have you been filling out your journals every day?" Answer any questions they may have about the journals. Encourage them to keep filling them out. Distribute more journal pages to students who need them.

2. Read aloud Chapter 1 of *The Survival Guide for Kids with LD* ("Why Do Some People Have LD?," pages 7–10) or play the audio cassette.

3. Distribute the "What Are Learning Differences?" handout. Say, "You all have one thing in common: you have LD. But your learning differences are not all alike. Today we're going to find out more about what it means to have LD. We're going to really think about how LD affects your life." Read through the handout. Allow time for questions and discussion.

4. Distribute the "How LD Affects Me" handout and pencils. Say, "It's important to understand how your learning differences can affect some of the things you do. When you don't understand, it's easy to get frustrated and angry with yourself.

"This handout lists pairs of choices. As I read each pair, circle or check the one that is like you *most of the time*. For some of the choices, it may be hard to decide. Just do the best you can."

NOTE: If you are working with older students, you may want to let them complete the handout independently.

5. Write the category headings from the hand-out—"Difficulty with Reading," "Difficulty with Spelling and Writing," etc.—on the board or flip chart. Beneath each heading, write "Yes" and "No."

Read through the handout again and ask for a show of hands as you read each choice. Put tally marks by "Yes" for each student who circled the first statement in each pair. Put tally marks by "No" for each student who circled the second statement.

When you are finished, guide the students to see that they have similarities and differences. This activity builds group cohesiveness. Students learn that some things are difficult for them and for their peers. You might say, "Now you know that there are people who can really understand your learning differences. Some of them are in this group."

6. **Optional:** Read aloud Chapter 4 of *Josh: A Boy with Dyslexia* (pages 16–19). Or read from an alternate title from the Children's Literature section. Allow time for questions and discussion.

7. End the session by thanking the students for having the courage to share more about their LD. Remind them to keep giving themselves—and each other—"I Am, I Can" messages; to continue writing in their journals; and to bring their folders to the next session.

SESSION 3

What Are Learning Differences?

People with learning differences are intelligent. Some are VERY smart. This can be confusing, because in school they might not work up to their intelligence in some areas. Because they have learning differences, their brains sometimes mix up the information they receive.

Your brain is like a gigantic file cabinet. All of the information is stored in files in the drawers. Your learning differences can misplace the files, mix up the files, or cause the drawers to get stuck so you can't get the information you are trying to find. But you are NOT dumb. If you were, your file cabinet would be empty!

Every person with LD is different. Some have a hard time doing one or two things. Some have a hard time doing many things. These are some of the things people with LD might have trouble with. See which ones sound like you.

Difficulty with Reading

You don't like to read. Letters like "b," "d," "p," and "q" often look alike to you. You know a word one time and forget it the next. Sometimes you skip words and lines on a page, or you put letter sounds into words that aren't there. You get confused when someone asks you questions about what you have read.

Difficulty with Spelling and Writing

You learn how to spell words, but you forget them later. You can't remember if the word "they" is spelled "thay," "thae," or "thea." You have poor handwriting. Even when you think it looks neat, the spacing is wrong and other people can't read it. Your ideas are good, but you have a lot of trouble writing them down.

What Are Learning Differences? continued

Difficulty with Math

You put numbers in the wrong place, or you forget what step to do in a long math problem. In word problems, you don't know if you should add, subtract, multiply, or divide. You could put down the same answer to four different problems and not notice that you have done this. Sometimes you reverse numbers. It seems like you will never be able to remember all of the math facts.

Difficulty with Memory

You often forget what adults tell you to do. You can't remember what a word looks like when it is erased or taken away. You forget phone numbers and addresses. You say "What?" and "I don't remember" a lot. You forget the rules to games you play often.

Difficulty with Paying Attention

It is hard to focus on your assignments. You are distracted by noises or what others are doing. Many times you interrupt people when they are talking. Adults often tell you to pay attention.

Difficulty with Getting and Staying Organized

Many times you can't find your homework, or you leave it at home. You often misplace things, and you forget where you put them. Your bedroom is messy, and when you go to clean it up, you don't know where to start. At school, your locker or desk has everything just jammed in.

Session 3

What Are Learning Differences? continued

Difficulty with Directions, Time, and Space

You get left and right confused. You can't remember if New York is east or west. You have trouble putting months of the year in order or knowing what season certain months go with. It is hard to copy things from a distance or from up close, like problems from a math book. Learning to tell time was difficult for you.

Very Active

Your hands need to fiddle with things. You have trouble sitting still. You often rock back and forth in your chair. Many times you are told to sit down. Sometimes you get in trouble for talking too much, acting silly, or interrupting.

Very Quiet

You'd rather watch games than play them. Many people say that you are very quiet and serious. You try to keep people from finding out about your learning differences.

Difficulty with Physical Education

You have trouble with team sports. You get the rules mixed up, you make mistakes, and you are often picked last for teams. When you were younger, you had trouble learning to ride a bike. You knock things over or bump into things. You feel clumsy.

Remember:

Just because you have learning differences doesn't mean you are dumb. It doesn't mean you can't learn. You just learn differently. Your teachers and parents need to help you learn in ways that are right for you.

Session 3

SESSION 3

How LD Affects Me

As you read each pair of statements, circle or check the one that is like you *most of the time*.

Difficulty with Reading

☐ Reading is often difficult for me. It takes a lot of hard work for me to do well.

☐ Reading is very easy for me. It does not take a lot of effort to do well.

Difficulty with Spelling and Writing

☐ I forget how to spell many words. It is very hard for me to put my ideas on paper.

☐ I can spell words very easily. I have very little trouble writing sentences and paragraphs.

Difficulty with Math

☐ It is hard for me to remember math facts. Doing story problems and math problems is hard for me.

☐ I don't have trouble doing my math work on my own.

Difficulty with Memory

☐ I often forget words and things that have been written or said.

☐ I hardly ever forget words and things that have been written or said.

How LD Affects Me continued

Difficulty with Paying Attention

☐ It is hard for me to pay attention.

☐ It is easy for me to pay attention.

Difficulty with Getting and Staying Organized

☐ I have trouble keeping my things organized at home and at school.

☐ It is easy for me to keep my things organized.

Difficulty with Directions, Time, and Space

☐ I have trouble remembering directions or copying things.

☐ It is easy for me to remember directions or to copy things.

Very Active

☐ I have trouble sitting still.

☐ It is easy for me to sit still and concentrate.

Very Quiet

☐ I would rather watch than play.

☐ I would rather play than watch.

Difficulty with Physical Education

☐ Most things in gym are hard for me and I don't enjoy it.

☐ Gym is a lot of fun for me and I don't have trouble with it.

Session 3

How Learning Happens

LD Awareness Focus

Students state one way in which learning differences affect learning.

Self-Esteem Focus

Students write about and illustrate one of their individual strengths and a strength of one peer.

Materials Needed

Handouts

- "How Learning Happens" (pages 33–34)
- "We All Have Strengths" (page 35)

Supplies

- Pencils, markers, and crayons, enough for all students
- *The Survival Guide for Kids with LD*
- **Optional:** *The Survival Guide for Kids with LD* audio cassette
- **Optional:** *Josh: A Boy with Dyslexia* or any other book of your choice from the Children's Literature section (pages 127–142)

The Session

1. Welcome the students back to the group and allow a short time for sharing. You might simply ask, "Does anyone have anything they want to say or tell the group?" This gives them the opportunity for informal conversation.

Some of the children may talk about serious things, and some may just want to tell the group about something they did they day before. Some may choose to sit quietly. However, if you do this activity consistently, all of the children eventually will begin talking to one another. Sharing time is a powerful way to continue to solidify the group.

2. Distribute the "How Learning Happens" handout. Say, "This is a diagram of your brain. Today we will find out how the brain allows everyone to learn. We'll also learn what happens in your brain if you have LD. It's important to understand that when you have LD, *there is nothing wrong with your brain*. It just works in a different way.

"Your brain is something like a file cabinet. It stores information. If you were dumb, or if your brain didn't work, your file cabinet would be completely empty and it would be locked up. Now, we know that people with learning differences have file drawers that are full of information. So they can't possibly be dumb. What happens is that the files sometimes get misplaced or put in the wrong drawers. Sometimes, when LD is really getting in the way, the drawers may get temporarily stuck. It takes a lot of patience and effort to put the files back where they belong or to unstick the drawers."

Read through the handout. Allow time for questions and comments.

3. Read aloud Chapter 2 of *The Survival Guide for Kids with LD* ("Why Is It Hard for Kids with LD to Learn?," pages 11–15) or play the audio cassette. Afterward, invite the students to share their ideas about how and where learning breaks down for them.

4. Next, invite the students to tell the group about ways to learn that work for them. Some of these may already be listed on page 15 of *The Survival Guide for Kids with LD;* others may be new ideas. Write down any new ideas the children share with you.

5. Distribute the "We All Have Strengths" handout and pencils, markers, or crayons. Say, "Write your name on one of the characters. Then, on the other character, write the name I will give you. I want you to keep the second name a secret until the next session. Let's all agree to do that." Assign each student the name of another student in the group. You may want to whisper the name or write it on a slip of paper and give it to the student to copy on the handout.

Say, "In the space under the character with your name, write or draw something that is one of your personal strengths. This should be something you know very well or do very well."

"Next, in the space under the character with the other person's name, write or draw something that is one of his or her personal strengths." Allow time for the students to complete this activity, then collect the handouts for use in the next session.

6. **Optional:** Read aloud Chapter 5 of *Josh: A Boy with Dyslexia* (pages 20–26). Or read from an alternate title from the Children's Literature section. Allow time for questions and discussion.

7. End the session by thanking the students for their hard work. Remind them to keep secret the identity of the student whose strength they wrote or drew about today; to continue writing in their journals; and to make sure to bring their folders to the next session.

SESSION 4

How Learning Happens

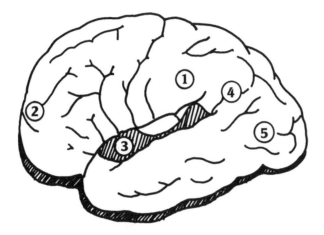

1. Concentration, judgment

2. Organizes thoughts

3. Forms sentences, remembers music, understands spoken words

4. Remembers words

5. Recognizes and organizes what you see

How Learning Happens continued

Input

When you learn, information gets into your brain through one or more of your five senses. Your five senses are:

1. sight   2. hearing   3. taste   4. smell   5. touch

Most of the information you learn in school goes into your brain through your first two senses, sight and hearing.

Attention

Your brain must pay attention to the information that comes through your senses. If you aren't paying attention, you won't keep much of the information that your senses bring to your brain.

Memory, Perception, and Organization

Your brain must figure out what the information means. Some of the information is stored in your **memory.**

Your brain must have **perception** (understanding) of the information. It must be able to **organize** the information and decide what, if anything, your body needs to do about it.

It is in these three areas of learning—memory, perception, and organization—that LD mixes things up and gets in the way.

Output

Information doesn't just go into your brain. It also comes out of your brain. To communicate the information in your brain, you can talk, write, or move your body.

Teachers measure what you know by looking at your **output.** At school, output usually means talking or writing. Some students with LD need different ways to show what they know.

Session 4

SESSION 4

We All Have Strengths

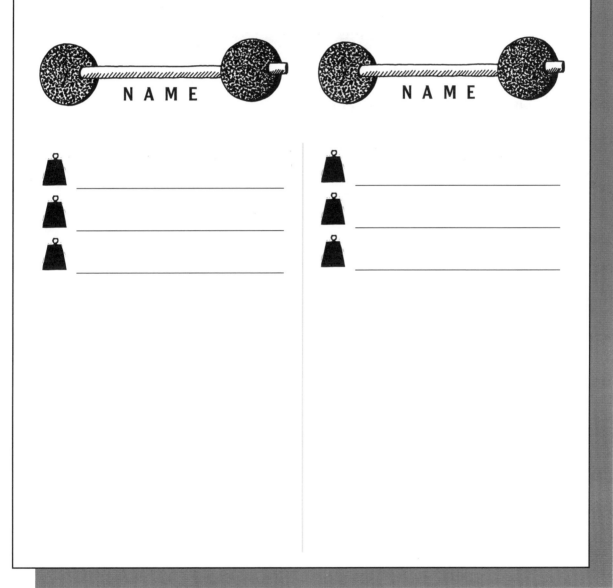

N A M E   N A M E

Understanding My LD

LD Awareness Focus

Students match their learning difference to one of the five types of learning differences. They learn several LD-related terms and their meanings

Self-Esteem Focus

Students reinforce their personal strengths and give each other positive affirmations.

Materials Needed

Handouts

- "LD Language" (pages 38–39)

Supplies

- Pencils, enough for all students
- Whiteboard, chalkboard, or flip chart; marker or chalk

- "We All Have Strengths" handouts saved from Session 4

- *The Survival Guide for Kids with LD*

- **Optional:** *The Survival Guide for Kids with LD* audio cassette

- **Optional:** *Josh: A Boy with Dyslexia* or any other book of your choice from the Children's Literature section (pages 127–142)

The Session

1. Welcome the students back to the group.

2. Distribute the "We All Have Strengths" handouts from Session 4. Invite the students to read aloud what they wrote about themselves and their strengths (or share their drawings). Then invite them to share what they wrote or drew about the other student whose name you assigned them during the last session. Afterward, thank the students for cooperating with the activity.

3. Read aloud Chapter 3 of *The Survival Guide for Kids with LD* ("Five Kinds of LD," pages 17–21) or play the audio cassette. Afterward, encourage the students to try to identify their own LD. Ask, "Where does learning break down for you? What kind of learning is hardest for you?" Allow time for discussion. Then ask the students, "Do you think you might have more than one type of LD?"

4. Read aloud Chapter 4 of *The Survival Guide for Kids with LD* ("How LD Got Its Name," pages 23–28) or play the audio cassette. Tell the students that they are going to learn more about "LD language"—some of the special words and phrases people use to talk about LD.

5. Distribute the "LD Language" handout and pencils. Divide the group into pairs. Assign each pair one or two terms from the list to define. Allow time for the students to work together to come up with their definitions. Make copies of *The Survival Guide for Kids with LD* available for students who need them.

Afterward, have the students share their definitions. Record their responses on the board or flip chart. Encourage the students to complete their "LD Language" lists by copying the answers you write.

NOTE: Depending on the skill level of your group, some of the students may find it difficult to copy from a distance. As an alternative, you might copy the group's definitions onto another "LD Language" handout, make photocopies, and distribute the copies during the next session.

After you finish recording the definitions, allow time for questions and discussion.

6. **Optional:** Read aloud Chapter 6 of *Josh: A Boy with Dyslexia* (pages 27–34). Or read from an alternate title from the Children's Literature section. Allow time for questions and discussion.

7. End the session by thanking the students for their cooperative work in pairs, and for sharing their definitions with the rest of the group. Say, "You're helping each other to learn and understand more about LD, and that's terrific." Remind them to keep giving themselves—and each other—"I Am, I Can" messages; to continue writing in their journals; and to bring their folders to the next session.

SESSION 5

LD Language

LD

_____

_____

_____

_____

LDA

_____

_____

_____

_____

Public Law 94-142

_____

_____

_____

_____

LD Language continued

Resource Room

_____

_____

_____

_____

Mainstreaming

_____

_____

_____

_____

LD Teacher

_____

_____

_____

_____

_____

Psychologist

_____

_____

_____

_____

Session 5

SESSION 6

My LD History

LD Awareness Focus

Students learn about the IEP and recall when they first began working in an LD program.

Self-Esteem Focus

Students identify some of their likes and dislikes, then compare their likes and dislikes with those of their peers.

Materials Needed

Handouts

There are no handouts for this session.

Supplies

- Construction paper or tagboard (any size to make a small poster), one piece per student

- Old magazines, catalogs, and/or newspapers

- Scissors, glue, and markers, enough for all students

- *The Survival Guide for Kids with LD*

- *The School Survival Guide for Kids with LD*

- **Optional:** *The Survival Guide for Kids with LD* audio cassette

- **Optional:** *Josh: A Boy with Dyslexia* or any other book of your choice from the Children's Literature section (pages 127–142)

- **Optional:** Overhead transparencies of your local special education forms; overhead projector

- **Optional:** Copies of the students' IEPs

The Session

1. Welcome the students back to the group and allow a few moments for conversation. Ask, "How many of you remember when you first started working with an LD teacher or resource room teacher to get special help for your learning differences?" Allow time for the children to think back on their experiences and respond. Then say, "Today you will find out just what had to happen for you to get help from an LD teacher. You'll learn more about the people who were involved, and you'll hear what needed to be done so you could receive special help."

2. Read aloud Chapter 5 of *The Survival Guide for Kids with LD* ("Getting Into an LD Program," pages 29–33) or play the audio cassette. Be sure to stress the information on pages 32–33 about the IEP.

Next, read aloud Chapter 6 of *The School Survival Guide for Kids with LD* ("You Can Handle Testing," pages 37–42).

NOTE: These chapters do an excellent job of simplifying the referral and testing procedures for students with LD.

Ask, "Who can remind the group what an IEP is? Why is it so important for each of you to have an IEP? How many of you have seen your own IEP?" Allow time for discussion.

3. **Optional:** Show overhead transparencies of your local special education forms. (You might prefer to show them at appropriate points during your readings from the Survival Guides.) Students are very interested in knowing that all of this important paperwork is done for each of them. They also appreciate having the mystery taken out of what can be for them a confusing and overwhelming process.

4. Say, "We have talked about how having LD is one way you are different from other people, and about how it is one way you are like one another. Now we're going to think more about differences.

"There are many things that make us all different from one another. For example, we don't all like the same things. We don't all dislike the same things, either."

Distribute construction paper or tagboard; magazines, catalogs, and newspapers; scissors, glue, and markers. While you are handing out the materials, say, "We're going to make posters about our likes and dislikes. Print your name at the top, draw a line down the middle, and label one side 'Likes' and the other side 'Dislikes.' Then look through the magazines, catalogs, and newspapers to find at least two or three things that illustrate your personal likes and dislikes. Cut them out and glue them onto your poster."

This activity will lend itself to natural conversation and increased awareness among the students that even though they have LD, they have unique personalities.

Afterward, invite the students to show their posters to the group and talk briefly about their likes and dislikes. Point out interesting differences and similarities, or ask the students to point them out.

The finished posters may be sent home or posted in the room.

5. **Optional:** If you have obtained copies of the students' IEPs, you might use the poster activity time to briefly show each student what his or her IEP looks like.

6. **Optional:** Read aloud Chapter 7 of *Josh: A Boy with Dyslexia* (pages 35–40). Or read from an alternate title from the Children's Literature section. Allow time for questions and discussion.

7. After the students have helped clean up, thank them for their hard work. Suggest that they take some time before the next session to talk to a friend who doesn't have LD and find out something they both like and/or dislike. Encourage them to keep writing in their journals, and remind them to bring their folders to the next session.

PART

2

Coping Skills

SESSION 7

Teasing

Coping Focus

Students describe a time when they were teased and how they responded. They rate the outcome as positive or negative.

Materials Needed

Handouts

- "Teasing Response Rating" (page 47)

Supplies

- Pencils, enough for all students
- Overhead transparency of "Teasing Response Rating" (page 47); overhead projector and marker

- *The Survival Guide for Kids with LD*
- **Optional:** *The Survival Guide for Kids with LD* audio cassette
- **Optional:** *Josh: A Boy with Dyslexia* or any other book of your choice from the Children's Literature section (pages 127–142)

The Session

1. Welcome the students back to the group and allow a few moments for conversation. Ask, "Have any of you ever met someone who is retarded?" Acknowledge responses. Then ask, "Have any of you ever been called 'retarded' by someone else?" Acknowledge responses. Finally, ask, "How many of you have ever wondered if having LD is the same as being retarded?" Ask for a show of hands. Then say, "Today you will find out that having LD is NOT the same as being retarded. You will learn what makes you different from people who are retarded."

2. Read aloud Chapter 6 of *The Survival Guide for Kids with LD* ("You Are Not Retarded!," pages 35–38) or play the audio cassette. Afterward, encourage each student to verbalize one way in which having LD is different from being retarded.

3. Ask, "How many of you have ever been teased?" Ask for a show of hands. Then say, "Teasing happens to everyone. Some teasing can be fun and doesn't hurt our feelings. But some teasing can hurt our 'I Am, I Can' signs. Some things we do can help make teasing stop. But other things we do don't seem to help at all."

4. Read aloud Chapter 9 of *The Survival Guide for Kids with LD* ("What to Do When Other Kids Tease You," pages 53–58) or play the audio cassette. Then say, "The next time we meet, we're going to practice ways to handle teasing situations. But today we're going to remember how we have handled teasing in the past."

5. Distribute the "Teasing Response Rating" handout and pencils. Allow time for students to complete the handouts. Make sure that they understand how to rate their responses on the bottom part of the handout.

Next, invite volunteers to share what they wrote on their handouts. Record their responses and ratings on the transparency for all to see. Afterward, allow time for discussion. You might ask questions like, "When does most of the teasing seem to happen?" "Where does it happen?" "When you look at the ratings, does it seem as if the people in this group are doing a good job of handling teasing?" "Why or why not?"

Collect the handouts for use in the next session. Say, "The next time we meet, we'll act out some of the teasing situations and come up with different ways to respond."

6. **Optional:** Read aloud Chapter 8 of *Josh: A Boy with Dyslexia* (pages 41–44). Or read from an alternate title from the Children's Literature section. Allow time for questions and discussion.

7. Thank the students for their cooperation. Tell them how glad you are that they are coming to the group. Encourage them to keep writing in their "I Am, I Can" journals, and remind them to bring their folders to the next session.

SESSION 7

Teasing Response Rating

WHO teased you? _____

WHEN did it happen? _____

WHERE did it happen? _____

WHAT did the person (or persons) tease you about? _____

_____

WHY do you think the person (or persons) teased you? Check one:

☐ Because they saw other kids doing it, and they wanted to be part of the group.

☐ Because they have been teased, and they wanted to hurt someone else the way they were hurt.

☐ Because they thought that if they made someone else feel bad, they would feel better.

☐ Because (write your reason): _____

_____

HOW did you respond to the teasing? _____

_____

WHAT happened then? _____

_____

Put an "X" on the line to rate your response:

It didn't work at all   It "kind of" worked   It worked out well

_____

I felt bad   I felt okay   I felt great

Responding to Teasing

Coping Focus

Students examine and role-play the steps necessary to respond appropriately and effectively to teasing.

Materials Needed

Handouts

- "Responding to Teasing Action Plan" (page 50)

Supplies

- "Teasing Response Rating" handouts saved from Session 7
- *The School Survival Guide for Kids with LD*
- **Optional:** *Josh: A Boy with Dyslexia* or any other book of your choice from the Children's Literature section (pages 127–142)

The Session

1. Welcome the students back to the group. Ask each student in turn to share one positive thing that has happened to him or her since the last group meeting.

Say, "Last time, we talked about teasing. Today you are going to learn how to make an action plan to deal with teasing situations. Before you can do that, you need to learn about ways to stick up for yourself."

2. Read aloud Chapter 14 of *The School Survival Guide for Kids with LD* ("You Can Stick Up for Yourself," pages 117–122). Allow time for questions and discussion. Make sure the students understand what "being assertive" means (page 120).

Next, read aloud Chapter 5 of *The School Survival Guide for Kids with LD* ("You Can Manage Mainstreaming," pages 31–36). Allow time for questions and discussion.

3. Distribute the "Responding to Teasing Action Plan" handout. Say, "This is an action plan for dealing with teasing situations. In a few minutes, we're going to act out some teasing situations and try this plan. There is no plan that is perfect and works every time. But if you give this plan a chance and keep using it, it WILL help you to deal with teasing."

Go over the handout with the students. Allow time for questions and discussion.

4. Divide the group into pairs. For each pair, verbally describe one of the situations students

wrote about on the "Teasing Response Rating" handouts from Session 7 (not their own). Say, "Come up with a way to respond to the teasing. Use the action plan. When you're ready, you'll act out your situation and your response."

While the students are working, go around to each pair and offer assistance where needed. For example, you may need to help them verbalize their thinking for step 2. If necessary, model using an assertive tone of voice and body language. Remind them to be sure to state how they feel, give the person a reason to stop, and walk away.

5. When the students are ready to proceed, ask, "Who would like to start?" Give each pair the opportunity to do their role play. If necessary, offer suggestions and encouragement. Instruct the rest of the group to watch for the steps in the action plan.

After all the role plays have been presented, thank the students for their hard work. Encourage them to use the action plan whenever anyone teases them.

6. **Optional:** Read aloud Chapter 9 of *Josh: A Boy with Dyslexia* (pages 45–48). Or read from an alternate title from the Children's Literature section. Allow time for questions and discussion.

7. Congratulate the students on their role plays. Encourage them to use the "Responding to Teasing" action plan whenever anyone teases them.

SESSION 8

Responding to Teasing Action Plan

1

STOP and count to five.

2

THINK about your choices:

▶ Will ignoring the teasing work?
▶ Can you just walk away?
▶ Are there friends around to help you?
▶ Do you need an adult to help you?
▶ Do you need to handle it yourself?

3

IF you need or want to handle it yourself:

▶ Stay calm.
▶ Be assertive. (*Remember:* Use a medium voice. Look the other person in the eye. Make suggestions, not demands. Don't make threats.)
▶ Say how you feel, give the person a reason to stop, and then walk away.

SESSION 9

Using I-Messages

Coping Focus

Students learn to create I-Messages to handle strong feelings.

Materials Needed

Handouts

- "I Get Angry or Frustrated When..." (page 54)
- "How to Send an I-Message" (page 55)

Supplies

- Pencils, enough for all students
- Whiteboard, chalkboard, or flip chart; marker or chalk
- *The School Survival Guide for Kids with LD*
- **Optional:** *Josh: A Boy with Dyslexia* or any other book of your choice from the Children's Literature section (pages 127–142)

The Session

1. Welcome the students back to the group. Ask, "Has anyone tried the action plan for teasing?" Allow time for students to tell their stories. Find out what happened; did the plan work for them? Congratulate the children for trying the plan and encourage them to keep using it.

2. Say, "Today we're going to learn how to handle strong feelings, especially anger and frustration. We're going to start by role-playing some situations that can happen in school and can cause strong feelings."

Choose two or more of the following situations to role-play. Ask for volunteers to role-play them with you. For each role play, continue until you get a reaction.

- Take the student's folder, paper, or pencil and refuse to give it back.

- Tease the student about his or her inability to do something.

- Cut in front of the student in line. Be rude about it.

- Copy the student's paper during a test.

- Tell the student that the rest of the class is going to play a game, but he or she won't be able to play.

- Start a false rumor about the student.

NOTE: Obviously, this activity depends on trust and good judgment. You don't want to take it too far, and you want to make sure that everyone understands that it's just a role play. Stop immediately if it seems that a student is genuinely hurt or upset.

3. Afterward, thank the students who volunteered to do the role plays with you. Ask them, "What were your feelings during the role plays?" Record their feeling words on the board or flip chart. Point out the similarities and differences among their feelings.

4. On the board or flip chart, list and discuss the ways the students responded during the role plays. For each response, ask the group "How many think this didn't work at all? How many think it 'kind of' worked? How many think it worked well?" Tally the students' ratings for each response.

5. Distribute the "I Get Angry or Frustrated When..." handout and pencils. Say, "Here are some examples of situations that can make you feel angry or frustrated." Read through the examples.

Then ask, "What are some things that can make you feel angry or frustrated? Try to think of at least two, and write them in the blank spaces." Allow time for students to write their examples. Afterward, invite volunteers to share what they have written.

6. Say, "There is a powerful way to handle times when you're feeling angry or frustrated. It works for many people in many different types of situations. You could use it to handle some of the teasing situations we have talked about."

Read aloud the section titled "Step 1: Tell the other person how you see the problem" in *The School Survival Guide for Kids with LD* (pages 124–125). Allow time for questions and discussions. Invite volunteers to give examples.

7. Distribute the "How to Send an I-Message" handout. Read through it with the students.

Then say, "Look back at your 'I Get Angry...' sheet. Pick one incident from this sheet. Think of an I-Message you could send about it." Give the students time to work on their I-Messages. Be available to help those who need assistance. Afterward, invite volunteers to share their I-Messages.

8. **Optional:** Read aloud Chapter 10 of *Josh: A Boy with Dyslexia* (pages 49–54). Or read from an alternate title from the Children's Literature section. Allow time for questions and discussion.

9. Thank the students for their hard work during this session. Encourage them to use I-Messages between now and the next session to handle strong feelings and respond to teasing. Remind them to bring their folders to the next session.

SESSION 9

I Get Angry or Frustrated When...

I'm on the playground and someone is chasing me or pushing me.

A friend promises to sit with me at lunch, but doesn't save me a place and ignores me.

I'm working in a group in the classroom and no one listens to my ideas.

The teacher explains an assignment that's due tomorrow, but I can't understand the explanation.

I tell my parents about my day, but they don't really listen.

_____

_____

_____

_____

_____

_____

_____

_____

Understanding LD, copyright © 1994 Susan McMurchie. Free Spirit Publishing Inc. Reproducible for classroom use only.

SESSION 9

How to Send an I-Message

1. Start your sentence with "I."

2. Tell the person HOW you feel.

"I feel _____ " OR

"I'm _____."

3. Tell the person WHAT he or she did that made you feel that way.

"I feel _____

WHEN YOU _____."

4. Tell the person WHY it bothers you.

"I feel _____

when you _____

BECAUSE _____."

Examples:

▶ "I feel mad when you take my book without asking because I still need to use it."

▶ "I feel frustrated when you give me something that is hard to read because my LD gets in the way."

▶ "I feel upset when you call me names because it isn't nice."

SESSION 10

Dealing with Negative Feelings

Coping Focus

Students learn positive ways to deal with sad, hurt, angry feelings.
They give themselves and their peers positive affirmations.

Materials Needed

Handouts

- "I-Message Rating" (page 59)

- "Strength Statements" (page 60)

- "Strength Statement Cards" (page 61)
  (NOTE: If possible, have these run off on
  oaktag or construction paper. Also, each
  student will need one card for each member
  of the group, so if your group has more than
  six students, you will need more than one
  handout per student.)

Supplies

- Pencils, enough for all students

- Scissors

- Letter or legal size envelopes, one per student

- Overhead transparency of "I-Message Rating"
  (page 59); overhead projector and marker

- A completed "Strength Statement Card" to
  use as an example

- *The Survival Guide for Kids with LD*

- **Optional:** *The Survival Guide for Kids with
  LD* audio cassette

- **Optional:** *Josh: A Boy with Dyslexia* or any
  other book of your choice from the Children's
  Literature section (pages 127–142)

The Session

1. Welcome the students back to the group and allow a few moments for conversation. Some students may mention that they tried sending an I-Message since the last session. Tell them that in just a few minutes they will have a chance to tell the group exactly what happened.

2. Distribute the "I-Message Rating" handout and pencils. If you used the "Teasing Response Rating" handout in sessions 7 and 8, you might point out that "I-Message Rating" handout is very similar to that one, and this is something they already know how to complete. Allow time for students to complete the handouts. Make sure that they understand how to rate their I-Messages on the bottom part of the handout.

Afterward, invite volunteers to share what they wrote on their handouts. Give them the opportunity to write their own "X" on the continuum line at the bottom of the transparency. Allow a few moments for discussion. You might ask questions like, "When do you seem to need I-Messages the most?" "Where do you need them?" "When you look at the ratings, does it seem as if I-Messages are working for the people in this group?" "Why or why not?"

NOTE: There may be some students who did not use an I-Message since the last session and won't have anything to report. You may want to ask them to make a verbal commitment to try this important technique before the next session. Then repeat this activity during that session. If necessary, quickly review the steps involved in using I-Messages, spelled out on the "How to Send an I-Message" handout (page 55).

3. Say, "In this group, we are learning to deal with many situations that often happen to people who have learning differences. We are also learning to deal with feelings that people with LD often have. It's important to know how we are feeling and why. We also need to know how to help ourselves and each other when we have sad, hurt, and angry feelings."

Read aloud Chapter 7 of *The Survival Guide for Kids with LD* ("How to Deal with Sad, Hurt, Angry Feelings," pages 39–45) or play the audio cassette. Afterward, have each student choose and verbalize one of the "Six Ways to Help Yourself Feel Better." Allow time for questions and discussion about the six ways.

If time permits, have each student try one of the "I Like Me" exercises described on page 43 of *The Survival Guide*.

4. Distribute the "Strength Statements" handout. Invite volunteers to read the statements. Ask, "How would hearing one of these statements make you feel about yourself? What if you heard it when you were feeling sad, hurt, or angry? Would it help you to feel better about yourself?"

Say, "We're going to practice giving and receiving some of these powerful statements. The secret to their power is the way they are given. You have to pick one that you believe really fits the person you want to give it to, and you have to say it like you really mean it. You have to say it *assertively*. This means using a medium voice and looking the other person in the eye."

5. Distribute the "Strength Statement Cards" handout and scissors. Show the group the "Strength Statement Card" you completed as an example. Say, "We're going to make these cards for each other. Start by cutting the cards apart. At the top of each card, write the name of a person in this group. Make one card for each person. Then pick a 'Strength Statement' from the handout that really fits that person. Write it on the card, and sign your name at the bottom. If you don't see a statement on the list that fits that person, you can write your own."

Allow time for students to complete the cards. Then have the students give the cards to one another, reading the statements aloud.

6. Distribute the envelopes. Say, "Put your cards in the envelope, and put the envelope in a safe place. Then, whenever you have sad, hurt, or angry feelings, take out your cards and look at them. Let them help you feel better."

7. **Optional:** Read aloud Chapter 11 of *Josh: A Boy with Dyslexia* (pages 55–61). Or read from an alternate title from the Children's Literature section. Allow time for questions and discussion.

8. Thank the students for sharing their feelings and supporting one another. Encourage them to keep writing in their "I Am, I Can" journals, and remind them to bring their folders to the next session.

SESSION 10

I-Message Rating

WHO did you send your I-Message to? _____

WHEN did you send your I-Message? _____

WHERE were you when you sent it? _____

WHY did you send your I-Message? _____

_____

_____

_____

WHAT did your I-Message say?

"I feel _____

when you _____

BECAUSE _____."

WHAT happened next? _____

_____

_____

_____

Put an "X" on the line to rate your I-Message:

It didn't work at all   It "kind of" worked   It worked out well

_____

I still felt bad   I felt better   I felt great

SESSION 10

Strength Statements

▶ I hope today is a good day for you.

▶ I'm glad you're in this group.

▶ Thanks for being my friend.

▶ I'm happy I know you.

▶ I would like to get to know you better.

▶ I like to be with you.

▶ I feel great when I'm with you.

▶ You're fun to be around.

▶ You're a good listener.

▶ You're a special person.

▶ You have a good sense of humor.

▶ You're a kind person.

▶ You're really good at _____.

▶ I like it when you _____.

▶ You helped me when you _____.

▶ You did a good job when you _____.

▶ _____.

▶ _____.

▶ _____.

SESSION 10

Strength Statement Cards

To: _____

Signed: _____

To: _____

Signed: _____

To: _____

Signed: _____

To: _____

Signed: _____

To: _____

Signed: _____

To: _____

Signed: _____

SESSION 11

School Stress

Coping Focus

Students learn ten ways to get along better in school. They practice two relaxation techniques and choose one that works best for them.

Materials Needed

Handouts

There are no handouts for this session.

Supplies

- *The Survival Guide for Kids with LD*

- *The School Survival Guide for Kids with LD*

- **Optional:** *The Survival Guide for Kids with LD* audio cassette

- **Optional:** *Josh: A Boy with Dyslexia* or any other book of your choice from the Children's Literature section (pages 127–142)

The Session

1. Greet the students and welcome them back to the group. Allow a few moments for students to share situations in which they have tried using I-Messages or some of the other coping strategies they have learned in the group. If anyone expresses frustration with a particular situation, encourage the group to brainstorm alternative solutions for the student to try.

2. Say, "One of our goals in this group is to work together to help you find ways to get along better in your life. You spend a big part of each day in school. Many students with LD have a hard time in school—not only with reading, writing, and math, but also with getting along with others.

"If you don't learn how to get along with others when you are in school, you might have a hard time being successful later in life, when you have to get a job and work with other people.

"Even though some of you might not like school, you still need to do your best to stay out of trouble and get along with others. Today we're going to learn ways to be more successful in school."

3. Read aloud Chapter 8 of *The Survival Guide for Kids with LD* ("Ten Ways to Get Along Better in School," pages 47–52) or play the audio cassette. Pause after reading each strategy and invite the students to comment on how important they think it is.

4. Say, "There is another time when many students with LD have trouble in school: on days when there is a substitute teacher. Let's find out how to make those days go more smoothly."

Read aloud page 135 of *The School Survival Guide for Kids with LD*. Allow time for questions and discussion.

NOTE: This page is from Chapter 17, "You Can Stay Out of Trouble." The rest of the chapter deals with more severe school problems that may or may not be appropriate to discuss with your group. Use your judgment to determine whether to share this information with your group.

5. Say, "Now we're going to go back to something we talked about a few minutes ago: ways to relax and cool off. Many adults use relaxation techniques to calm themselves down on hard days. What are some times when you might need to calm down, relax, and cool off?" Allow students to brainstorm situations in their lives when knowing how to relax could help them through a difficult or stressful time.

6. Repeat the two relaxation techniques from page 51 of *The Survival Guide for Kids with LD*. Divide the group into pairs or small groups. Say, "Pretend that you are in a stressful situation. Try each of the two relaxation techniques one time, then choose the one you feel most comfortable with. Coach each other through the techniques. It's important that when you leave here today, you will know one way to relax yourself that works for you." Allow time for students to try the techniques.

NOTE: Go around the room and monitor the students to make sure that they are doing the deep breathing as described in *The Survival Guide*.

Afterward, have each student tell the group which technique they feel most comfortable with and why.

7. **Optional:** Read aloud Chapter 12 of *Josh: A Boy with Dyslexia* (pages 62–67). Or read from an alternate title from the Children's Literature section. Allow time for questions and discussion.

8. Thank the students for agreeing to try the relaxation techniques. Encourage them to use their chosen technique whenever they need to relax and cool off in the days ahead. Remind them to bring their folders to the next session.

Making and Keeping Friends

Coping Focus

Students learn ten techniques for making and keeping friends.
They practice identifying how other people are feeling by observing
their facial expressions or body language.

Materials Needed

Handouts

- "Ten Tips for Making and Keeping Friends" (page 67)

Supplies

- Construction paper or tagboard (any size to make a small poster), one piece per student
- Old magazines, catalogs, and/or newspapers

- Scissors, glue, and markers, enough for all students
- *The Survival Guide for Kids with LD*
- *The School Survival Guide for Kids with LD*
- **Optional:** *The Survival Guide for Kids with LD* audio cassette
- **Optional:** *Josh: A Boy with Dyslexia* or any other book of your choice from the Children's Literature section (pages 127–142)

The Session

1. Welcome the students back to the group. Ask, "Has anyone tried their relaxation technique since the last session?" Allow time for students to tell about their experiences.

2. Say, "During the last session, we talked about ways to get along better in school. One very important skill we all need is knowing how to make friends. This will help us to get along better in school and in life. Everyone needs friends!

"There are things you can learn and practice that will help you make new friends and get along better with the friends you already have."

Read aloud Chapter 10 of *The Survival Guide for Kids with LD* ("Tips for Making and Keeping Friends," pages 59–61) or play the audio cassette. As you read the "10 Tips" on page 61, have the students give the "thumbs up" sign for each tip they believe is an important idea. They may raise their thumbs for as many tips as they like.

3. Distribute the "10 Tips for Making and Keeping Friends" handout. Say, "Here's a list of the ideas we just heard about. You may want to pick one or two to work on and see if they help you."

NOTE: Chapter 16 of *The School Survival Guide for Kids with LD* ("Eight Ways to Rescue Recess," pages 129–132) contains excellent ideas for handling recess. You may want to read this chapter to your group, depending on how old the students are and whether the school has recess. Then allow time for a brief discussion of the eight suggestions and what the students think of them.

4. Say, "There are reasons why people with LD sometimes have trouble getting along with others. As I read four reasons, see if you agree with them."

Read aloud Chapter 13 of *The School Survival Guide for Kids with LD* ("You Can Get Along with Others," pages 107–115). Pause after each reason to allow time for discussion. You might invite volunteers to describe times in their own life when they have said or done something without thinking; had trouble with talking and listening; had trouble with sports or games. Save discussion of Reason #4, "Trouble with Feelings," for the next activity in this session.

5. Ask, "How many of you have ever had trouble figuring out how other people were feeling?" Allow a few moments for students to describe their experiences. Afterward, say, "Sometimes we can figure out how people are feeling just by looking at them. We can tell if they are happy or sad, angry or busy by looking at their faces and their body language."

Make sure that everyone understands what "body language" means. Model some examples for the class.

- Someone putting hands on hips and giving a big sigh to show frustration or disappointment.

- Someone who is relaxed and smiling, friendly and approachable.

- Someone who is guarded and unapproachable—sitting or standing stiffly, with hands folded over chest.

- Someone who is very busy—leaning over desk, looking at paper, concentrating—and doesn't want to be disturbed.

- Someone who is restless, distracted, and bored.

6. Distribute construction paper or tagboard; magazines, catalogs, and newspapers; scissors, glue, and markers. While you are handing out the materials, say, "We're going to make posters about facial expressions and body language. Print your name at the top of the paper [or board]. Then look through the magazines, catalogs, and newspapers to find pictures of people who are showing different kinds of feelings. Look at their faces and their body language to see if you can determine what they are feeling. Help each other

out. Cut out the pictures and glue them onto your poster. Underneath each picture, write what you think the person is feeling."

When the students are finished with their posters, have them show them to the group and explain the feelings they identified. The finished posters may be sent home, posted in the room, or saved for future discussions about feelings.

7. **Optional:** Invite your school counselor, psychologist, or social worker to visit your group and talk about social skills. As preparation, you might have students write down one problem they have in getting along with others. They could present their problem to the counselor, psychologist, or social worker during the group, and everyone could benefit from what the expert has to say.

8. **Optional:** Read aloud Chapter 13 of *Josh: A Boy with Dyslexia* (pages 68–72). Or read from an alternate title from the Children's Literature section. Allow time for questions and discussion.

9. Thank the students for their hard work. Say, "During the days and weeks ahead, try to figure out how people in your life are feeling by looking at their faces or body language. See if this helps you to get along better with them." Remind the students to keep writing in their "I Am, I Can" journals, and to keep using I-Messages and relaxation techniques.

SESSION 12

10 Tips for Making and Keeping Friends

1. Watch other kids in class and on the playground. See if you can find some who play without teasing or fighting. They would probably make good friends.

2. Take part in games on the playground where kids line up to play and take turns.

3. Watch to see what the other kids like. Find out as much as you can about what they like. Then you can talk with them about the things they like.

4. Do not try to *make* other kids be your friends, especially the most popular ones. You might find good friends in students who are not part of the "in crowd." Is there someone who seems shy? Maybe that person is waiting for *you* to act friendly first.

5. Do not wander around the playground by yourself and hope someone will ask you to play. Instead, choose a game and ask someone to join you.

6. When you play with others, say nice things to them, take your turn, and be a good sport.

7. Do not show off or get into trouble to get noticed.

8. Most people like to talk about themselves. Ask other kids questions about what they like to do. Or ask them about their favorite TV shows, sports, or games.

9. Be friendly, share things, and do not tease. Treat other kids the way you want them to treat you. (That's right: This is the Golden Rule!)

10. Like yourself. Kids like other kids who like themselves.

PART

3

Self-Help Skills

SESSION 13

Asking for Help

Self-Help Focus

Students recognize the importance of asking for help. They practice a way
to ask and role-play situations when they might need help.

Materials Needed

Handouts

- "Asking for Help" (page 73)
- "Times When You Might Need Help" (page 74)

Supplies

- Pencils, enough for all students
- Whiteboard, chalkboard, or flip chart; marker or chalk
- *The School Survival Guide for Kids with LD*
- **Optional:** *Josh: A Boy with Dyslexia* or any other book of your choice from the Children's Literature section (pages 127–142)

The Session

1. Welcome the students back to the group. Allow a few moments for conversation.

2. Say, "In this group, you are learning many ways to help yourself. You are also learning ways to help and support one another. Today we're going to learn something that's very hard for some people to do. We're going to learn how to ask for help."

Ask, "What is one time when you might need to ask someone else for help?" Allow time for discussion.

Ask, "Has there ever been a time when you didn't ask for help, but you found out later that you should have?" Allow time for discussion. Make sure that students recognize why they should have asked for help. You might want to follow up their examples by asking, "What happened because you didn't ask for help? What do you think might have happened if you had asked for help?"

3. Ask, "Why is it sometimes hard to ask for help?" Allow time for discussion. Then say, "There will be many times when you need to ask an adult for help. You need to know when to ask, who to ask, how to ask, and what to do with the help you get."

Read aloud Chapter 8 of *The School Survival Guide for Kids with LD* ("You Can Get Help from Adults," pages 49–57). Pause frequently to allow for questions and discussion.

NOTE: Be sure to emphasize "Be Honest about Your LD" on page 53. Students need reassurance and encouragement to tell important people in their lives about their learning differences. This is a very important step in their self-advocacy.

4. Distribute the "Asking for Help" handout and pencils. Introduce the handout by saying, "It's important to have a plan for asking other people for help. If we have a plan, we can practice it until we feel comfortable with it. This makes it easier to ask for help when we really need it."

Go through the handout with the students. Read the steps aloud, or ask for volunteers to read them. Make sure the students understand each step. Model any that you feel need modeling.

5. Distribute the "Times When You Might Need Help" handout. Invite volunteers to role-play the situations. If some students are reluctant to participate, give them special encouragement. You want *all* of the students to practice asking for help in the safe, supportive environment of the group.

As the students role-play the situations, write down the different phrases they use on the board or flip chart. Afterward, have the students complete their "Asking for Help" handouts by writing down some of the phrases from the role plays.

6. **Optional:** Read aloud Chapter 14 of *Josh: A Boy with Dyslexia* (pages 73–80). Or read from an alternate title from the Children's Literature section. Allow time for questions and discussion.

7. Thank the students for their cooperation during this session. Encourage them to use the self-help skills they have learned today in the coming days and weeks. Remind them to keep writing in their "I Am, I Can" journals, and to bring their folders to the next session.

SESSION 13

Asking for Help

1. Ask yourself, "Am I working as hard as I can?"

2. Try a relaxation technique.

3. Try doing the work again.

IMPORTANT

You must try to do the work before asking for help. Try to do at least two problems or questions. If you still can't do the work after trying at least two problems or questions, then...

4. Ask for help from someone you trust. Be polite and assertive.

5. Tell the person EXACTLY what you need help with. Don't just say, "I don't get it."

6. After the person helps you, be sure to say, "Thank you."

Examples:

▶ "I'm confused about _____. Would you please help me?"

▶ "I'm frustrated with _____. Would you please help me?"

▶ "I'm _____
_____"

▶ "I'm _____
_____"

SESSION 13

Times When You Might Need Help

1

You are having a hard time trying to finish a project in art class.
Show how you would ask your friends or teacher to help you finish.

2

You get into trouble with your friends.
Show how you would ask your brother or sister to help you solve your problem.

3

You want your friend to teach you how to play a game.
Show how you would ask for help.

4

You are having a hard time reading the social studies test.
Show how you would ask your teacher for help.

5

You are having a hard time with your homework assignment.
Show how you would ask your parents for help.

6

You are having a hard time getting along with your math teacher in class.
Show how you would ask your parents or your LD teacher for help.

Setting Goals

Self-Help Focus

Students develop a short-term goal-setting plan and complete goal-setting contracts.

Materials Needed

Handouts

- "Goal-Setting Steps" (pages 78–79)
- "I Am Doing It!" (pages 80–81)
- "How Am I Doing?" (page 82)

Supplies

- Pencils, enough for all students
- **Optional:** A large chart showing the "Goal-Setting Steps"
- **Optional:** *Josh: A Boy with Dyslexia* or any other book of your choice from the Children's Literature section (pages 127–142)

The Session

1. Welcome the students back to the group. Ask, "Did anyone ask for help since the last time we met? What happened?" Allow time for students to share their experiences. Congratulate all students who asked for help, and encourage the group to keep trying.

2. Ask, "Who can tell me what a goal is?" Some students may respond by describing goals made in sports such as hockey, football, or soccer. Acknowledge their answers. If no one introduces the idea of personal goals, lead the group to the understanding that a goal is something a person decides is worth achieving, then makes an effort to achieve.

Ask, "Who has worked hard at something—in sports, at school, at home, or anywhere else—and then achieved what you wanted to do? How did you feel when you reached your goal? Why do you think you were able to achieve it?" Allow time for responses and discussion.

3. Broaden the discussion about goals by clarifying and discussing the difference between academic and social goals. Elicit ideas from the group on realistic, attainable goals versus nonrealistic, impossible goals. Discuss the difference between goals a child might have and goals an adult might have.

4. Ask, "Do you think that the people in this group might all have different goals?" Emphasize that this is one reason why goals are often called "personal goals." Each person has his or her own goals—things he or she wants to achieve. Invite volunteers to share one or two of their personal goals.

5. Distribute the "Goal-Setting Steps" handout. Say, "Your Individual Education Plan (IEP) lists goals for your LD program. These are goals that your parents and teachers worked together to write for you. Together, your goals make up a plan for what your parents and teachers hope you will achieve after working hard.

"There will be many times in your life when you will need to set your own goals. Some goals can be reached in a short amount of time, and some goals take longer to achieve. But no matter what type of goal you set for yourself, there are certain steps you must take in order to reach it."

Go over the steps on the handout with the group. You may find this easier to do if you have written the steps on a large chart that can be posted in the room.

Following are suggestions for points you may want to emphasize as you present each step and invite discussion.

- STEP 1: BEGIN. The student must decide what to strive for. The goal should be something that the student can actually achieve. It must be something that can be measured. For example, instead of saying, "I want my spelling to be better," the student needs to say, "My goal is to get only one or two wrong on my spelling test next week."

- STEP 2: MAKE A PLAN. Emphasize the importance of really thinking a plan through. Explain to the students that they should know who can help them and what things they might need to work toward their goal. Encourage them to visualize themselves working on their goal.

- STEP 3: ESTIMATE. Students need to understand how important this step is. The goal they set must not be too high or too low. (Many students tend to overestimate or underestimate.) Stress the need to set goals that are realistic...and worth striving for.

- STEP 4: RECORD. Students must write a positive statement asserting that the goal WILL be achieved. Using an I-statement with a verb ending in "-ing" is a positive way to accomplish this step. Reinforce the power of visualization—of "seeing" oneself reach the goal. Example: "I am working on my spelling."

- STEP 5: SET THE TIME. Encourage students to begin with meaningful short-term goals that can be achieved fairly quickly. This builds success and the desire to continue setting goals.

- STEP 6: DO IT! All students, not just those with LD, need support and encouragement to reach their goal. It's a good idea to send a note or newsletter to parents and classroom teachers explaining that your group is currently working on goal-setting and asking for their help. You might suggest that they ask the students to describe their goal, periodically check on their progress, ask them to re-read their goal statement, and generally keep track of how they are doing. They might also remind the students to visualize their goal.

- STEP 7: EVALUATE. After reaching (or not reaching) their goal, students should evaluate their progress and performance. Adults (parents, teachers) should also evaluate students' efforts and results. Students who did not reach their goal should think about why they didn't reach it and what they could do next time to improve their chances of success. Students who did reach their goal should receive positive affirmation for their hard work.

6. Distribute the "I Am Doing It!" handout and pencils. Explain to the group that these are goal-setting CONTRACTS. By completing the handout, they are agreeing to work toward a specific goal.

Allow time for students to complete the handout. Encourage them to help each other, and offer assistance when and where it is needed.

7. Distribute the "How Am I Doing?" handout. Say, "This chart will help you to keep track of your progress toward your goal. Each time you work on your goal, write down the date and what you did. You should try to write something down every day. That will remind you to keep working on your goal."

8. **Optional:** Read aloud Chapter 15 of *Josh: A Boy with Dyslexia* (pages 81–85). Or read from an alternate title from the Children's Literature section. Allow time for questions and discussion.

If you have been reading *Josh* since the group began, you have now finished the book. Thank the students for sharing it with you and congratulate them for paying close attention.

9. Thank the students for their cooperation during this session. Encourage them to keep working on their goals. Tell them that you'll be talking about goals again the next time you meet, and explain that they should be sure to bring their "I Am Doing It!" contracts and "How Am I Doing?" progress sheets to the next session.

SESSION 14

Goal-Setting Steps

Step 1: Begin

▶ What do you want to strive for?

▶ What do you want to accomplish?

▶ What do you want to improve?

TIP: Your goal should be realistic. It should be something you can really achieve.

Step 2: Make A Plan

▶ When will you start?

▶ Who will you ask to help you?

▶ What will you need to reach your goal?

TIPS: Start on your goal as soon as you can. Don't put it off! Make lists of people who can help you and things you need. Visualize yourself working on your goal.

Step 3: Estimate

▶ How much can you do right now?

▶ Is your goal realistic? Is it too hard or too easy?

▶ Is your goal something that is important to you? Does it mean something to you personally?

TIP: If your goal is too hard, you might get frustrated. If it's too easy, it might not seem very important. Your goal should feel "just right"—something you can really do, and something that will make a difference in your life.

Goal-Setting Steps continued

Step 4: Record

▶ Finish this sentence: "I am _____ing _____."

▶ Imagine yourself reaching your goal.

TIP: Remember that you are making a commitment to reach your goal. You are promising yourself that you will do your best to achieve what you have set out to do.

Step 5: Set the Time

▶ Finish this sentence: "I will reach my goal by _____."
                                                    DATE

▶ Make sure that the date you set is realistic.

TIP: Think about other things you are doing right now. What other commitments do you have? Do you have time to work on your goal? If your goal conflicts with other things you are doing, you might get frustrated and give up.

Step 6: Do It!

▶ Keep track of how you are doing.

▶ Keep imagining yourself reaching your goal.

TIP: Tell yourself, "This is something I am doing for myself. This goal is important to me. I will keep working on it until I reach it."

Step 7: Evaluate

▶ Review what you set out to accomplish.

▶ Think about how you feel.

▶ If you reached your goal: Congratulate yourself and thank the people who helped you.

▶ If you didn't reach your goal: Try to figure out why you didn't reach your goal. What can you do differently about the next goal you set for yourself?

TIPS: If you didn't reach your goal, this doesn't mean that you failed. You still accomplished a lot. You set a goal for yourself, and you worked hard to achieve it. You learned a lot, and you can use what you learned the next time you decide to work toward a goal.

Session 14

SESSION 14

I Am Doing It!

Step 1: Begin

I want to: _____

_____

Step 2: Plan

I will start: _____

I will ask these people to help me:

_____   _____

_____   _____

_____   _____

I will need these things:

_____   _____

_____   _____

_____   _____

I Am Doing It! continued

Step 3: Estimate

I can do these things right now:

_____   _____

_____   _____

_____   _____

> I feel confident that my goal is realistic.

Step 4: Record

I am _____ing _____.

Step 5: Set the Time

I will reach my goal by _____.
                              DATE

Signed: _____
              YOUR SIGNATURE

Session 14

SESSION 14

How Am I Doing?

My goal: _____

The date when I will reach my goal: _____

Date	What I Did
_____	_____
_____	_____
_____	_____
_____	_____
_____	_____
_____	_____
_____	_____
_____	_____
_____	_____
_____	_____
_____	_____
_____	_____
_____	_____

Overcoming Roadblocks

Self-Help Focus

Students review the goal-setting steps and identify an obstacle which may prevent them from reaching their goals.

Materials

Handouts

- "Roadblocks and Solutions" (page 85)

- "I Am Doing It!" (Session 14, pages 80–81)

- "How Am I Doing?" (Session 14, page 82)

Supplies

- Pencils, enough for all students

- Overhead transparency of "Goal-Setting Steps" handout from Session 14 (pages 78–79); overhead projector

- **Optional:** Any book of your choice from the Children's Literature section (pages 127–142)

The Session

1. Welcome the students back to the group. Ask, "Did you remember to bring your 'I Am Doing It!' and 'How Am I Doing?' handouts?" Invite the students to tell the group how they are doing with their goals. Are they following their contract? Are they recording their progress? Congratulate the students who reached their goals.

NOTE: Be sure to affirm *all* of the students for *any* effort they have made—even if they forgot to bring their handouts, even if they didn't reach their goal.

2. Say, "If you didn't reach your goal, it's important to figure out why. What stood in your way? What was your roadblock? Once you identify your roadblock, you can figure out how to avoid it the next time you set your goal. Even if you reached your goal this time, you might run into a roadblock next time, so we all need to learn about roadblocks and how to avoid them."

Divide the group into small groups for brainstorming. Distribute the "Roadblocks and Solutions" handout and pencils. Say, "Think of any roadblocks that kept you from reaching your goal, or that might keep you from reaching goals in the future. Then work together to come up with a solution for each roadblock. Be creative and accept all ideas. Record them on your handout." Allow time for students to complete the handout.

3. Have each group share their roadblocks and solutions. Point out the similarities and differences in their responses. As the students describe their roadblocks and solutions, record them on a piece of paper.

NOTE: Consider copying or typing your notes to give to the students during the next session, so they will have a list of roadblocks and solutions for future reference.

4. Use the "Goal Setting Steps" transparency to review the steps involved in setting a goal. Make sure that all of the students understand all of the steps. Allow time for questions and discussion if some students appear to need additional help and clarification.

5. Distribute the "I Am Doing It!" and "How Am I Doing?" handouts. Have the students set another short-term goal to work on. Students who didn't reach the goal they set during the last session may want to try that goal again, with modifications, or they may want to set a new goal. Students who did reach the goal they set during the last session should set a new goal, perhaps a little more challenging than the last one.

6. **Optional:** Read aloud from a book of your choice from the Children's Literature section. Allow time for questions and discussion.

7. Thank the students for their cooperation during this session. Encourage them to keep working on their goals and coming up with ways to avoid roadblocks.

NOTE: While future sessions of *Understanding LD* don't formally address goal-setting, this should be an ongoing process in the students' lives. Have extra copies of the "I Am Doing It!" and "How Am I Doing?" handouts available at all sessions. Take a few minutes at the start of each session to ask, "Who has reached a goal since the last session? Has anyone run into roadblocks they need help with?" Invite the students to describe their roadblocks and help each other by brainstorming solutions. This builds self-advocacy skills and peer relationships.

SESSION 15

Roadblocks and Solutions

Roadblock	Possible Solution

Being Successful

Self-Help Focus

Students identify the characteristics of a successful student.

Materials

Handouts

- "Successful Students" (page 89)

- "How Could You Handle It Better?" (page 90)

- "Ways to Help Yourself" (pages 91–92)

- "Choices" (page 93)

- Extra copies of "'I Am, I Can' List" (Session 1, page 15)

- Extra copies of "Strength Statements" (Session 10, page 60)

Supplies

- Pencils, enough for all students

- Whiteboard, chalkboard, or flip chart; marker or chalk

- **Optional:** Any book of your choice from the Children's Literature section (pages 127–142)

The Session

1. Welcome the students back to the group. Allow a few moments for conversation. You may want to encourage the students to reflect on the progress they are making because of the techniques they are learning in the group.

2. Say, "All of the things we do in this group are meant to help make your life easier and more successful. Today we are going to talk about success. Who can start by telling us what success means?" Allow a few moments for discussion.

Ask, "How many of you know students who are successful most of the time?" Invite a show of hands. Then say, "Let's talk about those students—but without giving their names. What are some of the things they do that help them to be successful most of the time?" Record responses on the board or flip chart.

NOTE: It is *very* important to emphasize that being smart is not always the same as being successful. Remind the students that they are as smart as anyone else in their class. Steer them toward describing specific actions successful students take, such as "They ask questions," not "They know a lot of things." If necessary, prompt them with a few examples from the "Successful Students" handout.

3. Distribute the "Successful Students" handout. Go through it with the students. Read the items on the list aloud, or ask for volunteers to read them. Then say, "The actions listed here—and the ones I listed on the board/flip chart—are things that most successful students do. If you can do them, too, you will be a successful student. And, when you are older, you will be a successful adult.

"No one expects you to do all of these things all of the time. Nobody does! But it's VERY important to understand that having learning differences doesn't mean you can't do these things. Your learning differences can't keep you from being successful."

4. Divide the group into pairs or small groups for brainstorming. Distribute the "How Could You Handle It Better?" handout and pencils. Say, "This handout describes four students who are NOT acting successful. Read each situation, then come up with a different, successful way for the student to act." Allow time for students to complete the handout. Afterward, invite students to share their ideas. Allow time for discussion.

5. Say, "You can help yourself to be more successful every day. Here is a list of things you can do and say to be more successful."

Distribute the "Ways to Help Yourself" handout. Say, "When you have LD, sometimes you need to remind the people around you. You don't have to say, 'Hey, I have LD! Did you forget?' Instead, you can say that you are having difficulty doing something. Most people won't mind if you say this—especially if they can see from your actions that you are trying to do your best."

Go over the handout with the students. Allow time for questions and discussion. Encourage the students to add their own ideas. Give extra copies of the "'I Am, I Can' List" and "Strength Statements" handouts to students who need them.

6. Divide the group into pairs. (Or keep them in the same pairs or groups they were in for Step 4 of this session.) Distribute the "Choices" handout. Say, "Now it's time to practice some of the things we have been learning today. This handout describes ten situations that can happen to you. Read them and pick one you'd like to try. Work with your partner to come up with a way to handle the situation. When you're ready, you'll act it out for the group."

While the students are working, go around to each pair and offer assistance where needed.

NOTE: Rather than letting the students choose which situation to work on, you may want to assign a different situation to each pair.

7. When the students are ready to proceed, ask, "Who would like to start?" Give each pair the opportunity to do their role play. Afterward, allow time for questions and discussion. Invite the students to contribute additional ideas and suggestions for handling each situation.

8. **Optional:** Read aloud from a book of your choice from the Children's Literature section. Allow time for questions and discussion.

9. Thank the students for their willingness to try new ways to be successful. Encourage them to use what they learned today between now and the next session. Remind them to bring their folders to the next session.

SESSION 16

Successful Students

▶ Want to do well

▶ Try

▶ Study

▶ Practice their skills

▶ Do their homework

▶ Get their work done on time

▶ Ask questions

▶ Ask for help when they need it

▶ Help others

▶ Listen carefully

▶ Pay attention

▶ Participate in class

▶ Cooperate

▶ Understand and accept that they sometimes make mistakes

▶ Are respectful

▶ Get to class on time

▶ Take their seats promptly

▶ Are organized

▶ Bring everything they need to each class

▶ (What else?) _____

▶ (What else?) _____

SESSION 16

How Could You Handle It Better?

1. Mrs. Smith asks John to name the capital of Wisconsin. He stares at her and shrugs his shoulders.

_____

_____

_____

2. Maria hates reading class. To avoid doing her work, she goes into her desk to pretend to find something. By the time she goes back to the reading book, she is a page or two behind.

_____

_____

_____

3. In math class, Mr. Williams asks Sam for answers to 6 x 8, 7 x 6, and 6 x 6. Sam can't think of the answers. He says, "I don't know."

_____

_____

_____

4. Matt's social studies teacher has just finished a review of all of the continents. The teacher went quickly because the class has a test the next day. Matt is confused. He says to his teacher, "This is impossible. I don't get it."

_____

_____

_____

Ways to Help Yourself

▶ Look at the teacher when he or she is talking.

▶ Smile at your teacher and nod your head to show that you understand something.

▶ When a teacher offers ideas to help you or corrects your mistakes, always say "Thank you."

▶ Give yourself at least one "I Am, I Can" statement every day. Give someone else at least one "Strength Statement" every day.

▶ Even if you didn't finish an assignment or you didn't like doing it, always hand in your work on time.

▶ If you don't understand something, ask the teacher if he or she can explain it differently using other words or examples.

▶ Another idea: _____

▶ Another idea: _____

Ways to Help Yourself continued

If you get stuck, try saying:

▶ "I understood what you said, but I can't remember everything I am supposed to do."

▶ "I listened to you, but I don't understand what I am supposed to do."

▶ "I can do all of the reading, but the writing will be difficult for me."

▶ "I have a very hard time with the reading."

▶ "I tried to listen to you, but I had a hard time concentrating."

▶ "I want to do a good job, and I will need more time to do the work."

▶ Another idea: _____

▶ Another idea: _____

REMEMBER:
Teachers don't get mad at students who try.

Session 16

SESSION 16

Choices

1. You didn't do your homework. Your teacher has just asked you about it. What do you say?

2. One of your classes is very boring to you. How should you act?

3. Your teacher is going too fast. How do you ask your teacher to slow down?

4. Your teacher made a mistake and accused you of breaking a class rule. When is the best time for you to talk about it with your teacher? What do you say?

5. You are late for class. What do you say to your teacher? When do you say it? How do you say it?

6. You don't understand something your teacher is explaining. How do you let your teacher know?

7. You feel that your teacher has insulted you. You are hurt and angry. What do you do?

8. You want extra help or extra credit. How do you ask for it?

9. There is a big project due in one week. You are feeling very pressured. What do you do?

10. The teacher gives everyone in your class an independent assignment. You must read a book and write a report. The assignment is due in two weeks. What do you do?

Learning to Concentrate

Self-Help Focus

Students formulate solutions to concentration problems.

Materials

Handouts

- "Concentration Problems" (page 97)
- "Concentration Roadblocks and Solutions" (page 98)

Supplies

- Pencils, enough for all students
- Overhead transparency of "Concentration Problems" (page 97); overhead projector and marker

- Examples of the learning materials described in Chapter 7 of *The School Survival Guide for Kids with LD:* a list of events that take different amounts of time to do (page 44); a calendar (page 44); index cards showing the different ways to tell time (page 45); blank clock faces drawn on index cards (page 46); materials for the clock game (pages 46–47)

- *The School Survival Guide for Kids with LD*

- **Optional:** Any book of your choice from the Children's Literature section (pages 127–142)

The Session

1. Welcome the students back to the group. Allow a few moments for conversation.

2. Say, "During our last meeting, we talked about success. Being able to concentrate is important to learning and success. Everyone has times when it's hard to concentrate. When you have learning differences, it can be even harder. Today we'll talk about some things that can get in the way of concentration, and we'll work together to come up with solutions to concentration roadblocks."

3. Distribute the "Concentration Problems" handout. Go through it with the students. Read the items on the list aloud, or ask for volunteers to read them. Invite the students to add their own ideas. Allow time for discussion.

4. Put the "Concentration Problems" transparency on the overhead projector. Ask each student to identify one or two of his or her most common concentration problems. Put tally marks on the transparency so students can see which problems seem to be most common within the group.

Summarize with a few comments based on the tally results. ("It seems as of most of the people in this group have problems with _____ and _____. But not many of you have problems with _____, and that's great!")

Say, "It's very important to know what things get in the way of your ability to concentrate. It's also important to know what to do when this happens. We're going to work on that next."

5. Divide the group into small groups. Distribute the "Concentration Roadblocks and Solutions" handout and pencils. If you used the "Roadblocks and Solutions" handout in Session

15, you might point out that the "Concentration Roadblocks and Solutions" handout is very similar to that one, and this is something they already know how to complete.

Give each group a concentration problem to solve. Choose problems that the group identified as being most common to them. It's all right to assign the same problem to more than one group. Allow time for students to complete the activity.

NOTE: Depending on the students' skill level, you may want to turn this into a timed brainstorming exercise. For each group, write a problem at the top of a piece of paper. Ask one person in each group to act as the recorder. Say, "You will have _____ minutes to come up with as many solutions to the problem as you can. The recorder should write down *all* of the answers. The more ideas you come up with, the better." Afterward, invite each group to share their ideas. Record them on a transparency or on a piece of paper.

NOTE: Consider copying or typing your notes to give to the students during the next session, so they will have a list of concentration roadblocks and solutions for future reference.

6. Say, "You might have noticed that some of the concentration problems are about time—for example, not having a set time to do homework, or putting something off when you should do it right away. Many students with LD have difficulty understanding time. Let's find out about some ways to master time."

Read aloud Chapter 7 of *The School Survival Guide for Kids with LD* ("You Can Master Time," pages 43–48). As you read the ideas in the chapter, show the examples of the learning materials you prepared for this session. If possible, give the students a chance to practice with them. If some of your students need extra help, you may want to let them borrow some of the materials until the next session.

7. **Optional:** Read aloud from a book of your choice from the Children's Literature section. Allow time for questions and discussion.

8. Thank the students for concentrating during this session. Encourage them to use what they learned today between now and the next session. Remind them to bring their folders to the next session.

SESSION 17

Concentration Problems

▶ people talking around me

▶ too much noise

▶ too many distractions

▶ daydreaming

▶ being tired

▶ being hungry

▶ not being organized

▶ personal problems

▶ trying to work with the TV or radio on

▶ not having a set time to do homework

▶ not having a set place to do homework

▶ putting off doing homework; saying "I'll do it later"

▶ not having the things I need to do homework (paper, pencils, ruler, calculator)

▶ don't like the subject I am working on

▶ can't understand the assignment

▶ Another concentration problem: _____

▶ Another concentration problem: _____

SESSION 17

Concentration Roadblocks and Solutions

Roadblock	Possible Solution

PART

Study Skills

SESSION 18

Getting Organized, Part 1

Study Skills Focus

Students identify organization problems and learn basic organization skills.

Materials

NOTE: If the students in your group already use class schedules and other tools for getting organized, you may want to use examples of their materials instead of or in addition to the handouts and transparencies listed for this session.

Handouts

- "Organization Problems" (page 104)
- "My Routine" (page 105)
- "Time Chart" (page 106), at least 6 for each student
- "Your Child is Learning..." (page 107)

Supplies

- Pencils, enough for all students
- Overhead transparency of "Organization Problems" (page 104); overhead projector and marker

- Overhead transparency of "My Routine" (page 105), partially filled in as an example (see page 9 of *The School Survival Guide for Kids with LD*) (NOTE: In your example, continue into the evening and show homework time)

- Overhead transparency of "Time Chart" (page 106), partially filled in as an example (see page 11 of *The School Survival Guide for Kids with LD*)

- *The School Survival Guide for Kids with LD*

- **Optional:** Any book of your choice from the Children's Literature section (pages 127–142)

The Session

1. Welcome the students back to the group. Ask, "Did anyone try a concentration solution since last time?" Invite students to talk about their experiences.

2. Say, "One of the concentration problems we talked about last time was the problem of not being organized. Who can tell me what it means to be organized?" Allow time for responses.

Afterward, say, "Today we're going to start learning ways to get organized. This is a problem for many people—students *and* adults. Not being organized can get in the way of success. Sometimes having LD can make it even harder to be organized."

Distribute the "Organization Problems" handout and pencils. Go through it with the students. Read the questions aloud, or ask for volunteers to read them. Invite the students to add their own ideas. Allow time for students to complete the handout.

3. Put the "Organization Problems" transparency on the overhead projector. Read each statement and ask for a show of hands at each "Often," "Sometimes," and "Never." Put tally marks on the transparency so students can see which problems seem to be most common within the group.

Summarize with a few comments based on the tally results. ("It seems as if most of the people in this group have problems with _____ and _____. That's okay, because we're going to learn what to do about those problems. We'll learn some new skills today and some the next time we meet.")

4. Read aloud pages 7–11 of Chapter 1 of *The School Survival Guide for Kids with LD* ("You Can Get Organized," pages 7–14). You'll read pages 12–14 during the next session. You may want to explain to the students that you'll be

learning about the first four of the "Eight Ways" this time, and the next four next time.

5. Distribute the "My Routine" handout. Say, "The first thing we're going to learn is how to make a daily routine for school. This will help you to remember what you are supposed to do at different times during the day."

Put the partially filled-in "My Routine" transparency on the overhead projector. Call the students' attention to the transparency and say, "Here is an example of how to complete your handout. Write down your schedule for each day of the school week. If you can't fill in a day or a square, just leave it blank."

Allow time for students to complete the handout. Be available to offer help where needed.

Afterward, invite volunteers to share their handouts with the class. Allow a few moments for discussion. Then ask questions like, "Do you think that having a routine will help you to be organized?" "Where would be a good place to keep your routine so you're sure to see it every day?"

NOTE: This handout is an especially powerful tool that can make a big difference in students' lives. First, it empowers them to take responsibility for their own work and activities. Second, it begins to free their parents from constantly having to remind them to do things. Third, when students learn to follow a routine and schedule their time, they discover that there really is time for everything, including things they want to do.

6. Distribute the "Time Chart" handout, one to each student. Say, "A lot of people have trouble using their time well. Suddenly it's the end of a day or a week and they haven't gotten anything done.

"It helps to keep track of how you spend your time. When you do this, you can start finding out if you're wasting time. Or maybe you're spending too much time on some things and not enough time on other things. Once you have a record of how you spend your time, you can start making decisions and changes."

Put the partially filled-in "Time Chart" transparency on the overhead projector. Say, "This is an example of how a time chart might look from breakfast through dinner. All we're going to do for now is write down how we have spent this day so far. Think of all the things you have done since you got out of bed. List them and write the amount of time you spent on each one."

Allow time for students to complete the handout. Afterward, ask questions like, "Are there any surprises on your time chart?" "Did you know you spent so much/so little time getting ready for school?" "Is there anything on your chart that you should spend more time doing? Less time doing?"

Distribute additional "Time Chart" handouts, enough for each student for at least a week.

Explain that they should complete one every day for a week (or until your next group meeting). Tell them to bring their filled-in charts to the next session.

7. **Optional:** Read aloud from a book of your choice from the Children's Literature section. Allow time for questions and discussion.

8. Thank the students for their cooperation and attention during this session. Remind them to bring their folders and their filled-in "Time Chart" handouts to the next session.

NOTE: Learning how to be organized takes time and practice. Students need ongoing support and encouragement to develop good habits in this important skill area. On page 107, you'll find a letter to photocopy and send home to parents, inviting them to get involved.

SESSION 18

Organization Problems

Think about each sentence. Then check "Often," "Sometimes," or "Never" to show how much this is a problem for you.

	Often	Sometimes	Never
1. I have trouble remembering what I am supposed to do at different times during the day.	☐	☐	☐
2. I have trouble turning assignments in on time.	☐	☐	☐
3. I have trouble using my time well during the day.	☐	☐	☐
4. I forget things I am supposed to do during the day.	☐	☐	☐
5. I do other things when I'm supposed to be doing my homework.	☐	☐	☐
6. I have trouble keeping track of my school materials.	☐	☐	☐
7. I have trouble remembering which room I'm supposed to go to for which class.	☐	☐	☐

SESSION 18

My Routine

Time	Mon	Tues	Wed	Thurs	Fri
:					
:					
:					
:					
:					
:					
:					
:					
:					
:					
:					
:					
:					
:					
:					
:					
:					
:					

SESSION 18

Time Chart

Day: _____

Activity   **Time**

_____   _____

_____   _____

_____   _____

_____   _____

_____   _____

_____   _____

_____   _____

_____   _____

_____   _____

_____   _____

_____   _____

_____   _____

_____   _____

_____   _____

_____   _____

Your Child Is Learning...

Dear Parent(s),

Getting organized is a problem for many people—students and adults, parents and teachers! Not being organized can get in the way of success. Sometimes having learning differences can make it even harder to be organized.

The students in our discussion group—including your son or daughter—are learning ways to organize their time and materials. Today we identified some organization problems that many people share, and we practiced using daily routine records and time use charts. The students are familiar with how to use these forms, but they will need reminders and encouragement to make them a habit. That's where *you* come in.

Ask your child to show you the forms we used today. Encourage your child to follow a routine and to track the way he or she uses time. (I've asked the students to fill out a week's worth of Time Charts.) During our next meeting, we'll be learning more organization skills. Be sure to check with your child at that time.

The more organized students become, the more they take responsibility for their own school work without being reminded by their parents. So there are benefits to *you* in helping your child get organized.

If you have any questions, feel free to call me at _____.

Sincerely,

Please sign and return the bottom part of this letter.

- -

I have read this letter and discussed it with my child.

_____   _____
(Parent signature)   (Date)

Getting Organized, Part 2

Study Skills Focus

Students continue learning ways to organize their time,
and also learn ways to organize their materials.

Materials

Handouts

- "Things to Do" (page 110), several copies for each student

- "Organizing Your Materials" (page 111)

- Extra copies of "My Routine" and "Time Chart" (Session 19, pages 105 and 106)

Supplies

- Pencils, one for each student

- Whiteboard, chalkboard, or flip chart; marker or chalk

- Overhead transparency of "Things to Do" (page 110), partially filled in as an example; overhead projector

- *The School Survival Guide for Kids with LD*

- **Optional:** Any book of your choice from the Children's Literature section (pages 127–142)

The Session

1. Welcome the students back to the group. Ask, "Who feels like they're making progress on getting organized?" Invite students to talk about their experiences.

2. Ask the students to take out the "Time Chart" handouts they completed since the last session. Ideally, each student will have a week's worth of completed forms; realistically, some might have only a few or none. Explain that even students who don't have any completed forms can still take part in the discussion. They can try to remember how they spent their time.

Begin a discussion by asking questions like, "What did you learn from your time charts?" "Were you surprised by anything you learned?" "What are you spending too much time doing?" "What are you spending too little time doing?"

Lead the students to the awareness that when they are organized—when they get their work done first and on time—they have more time for other things they want to do. Tell the students that today you'll be learning more ways to get organized.

3. Read aloud pages 12–14 of Chapter 1 of *The School Survival Guide for Kids with LD* ("You Can Get Organized," pages 7–14).

4. Distribute the "Things to Do" handout and pencils. Say, "Making a list of things to do is one of the best ways to get organized. You write down everything you want to get done on a certain day. Then you check off each item as you finish it. If you have things left over at the end of the day, you put them on your next day's list. Or maybe you decide that they're not that important, and you cross them off your list."

Put the partially filled-in "Things to Do" transparency on the overhead projector. Say, "Here is an example of how to complete your list. Now let's spend the next few minutes writing down the things we want to get done today."

Allow time for students to complete the handout. Be available to offer help where needed.

Afterward, invite volunteers to share their lists with the class. Allow a few moments for discussion. Then ask questions like, "Do you think that having a 'Things to Do' list will help you to be organized?" "What if you put the most important things at the top of your list? Would that help you to get them done?"

5. Say, "We've just talked about things we need to do. But sometimes we choose to do other things instead. We watch TV or talk on the phone, listen to music, or daydream. These time stealers keep us from getting our work done.

"Think about what happens when you sit down to do your homework. What are the time stealers that get in your way?" List students' responses on the board.

Afterward, ask each student, "What one thing from this list would be a good reward for getting your work done?" Put tally marks on the board to indicate student responses. Encourage students to do their homework first tonight, then reward themselves.

6. Distribute the "Organizing Your Materials" handout. Go through it with the students. Read the items aloud, or ask for volunteers to read them. Allow time for the students to respond to these ideas and consider how they might work for them. Invite the students to contribute ideas that aren't on the list. You may want to write their ideas on the board.

7. **Optional:** Read aloud from a book of your choice from the Children's Literature section. Allow time for questions and discussion.

8. Thank the students for their good work during this session. Tell them that you have extra copies of the handouts from the last session, and invite them to take some for future use. Encourage them to share the handouts with their parents and to keep using them every day.

SESSION 19

Things to Do

Day: _____

Check off
when done   **Activity**

_____   _____

_____   _____

_____   _____

_____   _____

_____   _____

_____   _____

_____   _____

_____   _____

_____   _____

_____   _____

_____   _____

_____   _____

_____   _____

_____   _____

_____   _____

_____   _____

SESSION 19

Organizing Your Materials

▶ Have a folder for each subject. Have a spiral notebook for each subject. Keep the spiral notebook in the folder.

▶ Color-code your folders and notebooks. Use different colors for different subjects. For example, if you use blue for math, your math folder and your math spiral notebook should both be blue.

▶ Have a separate folder for information to take home to your parents.

▶ Label each folder and notebook with this information:

— your name

— the subject

▶ When you get papers from your teacher—new handouts or information sheets, returned tests or papers—put them in the correct folder IMMEDIATELY.

▶ Keep your desk and locker neat. Don't just stash papers in them without organizing them. Recycle anything that doesn't have to go home or in a folder.

SESSION 20

Becoming a Better Learner

Study Skills Focus

Students learn specific techniques to facilitate learning. They commit to trying at least one technique they think might help them to become better learners.

Materials

Handouts

- "Draw Between the Lines" (page 115)
- "Crossword Puzzle Form" (page 116)

Supplies

- Pencils, enough for all students
- Whiteboard, chalkboard, or flip chart; marker or chalk (for use during small group discussions)

- 1–2 large pieces of poster paper, each with a heading that reads "Things We Can Do Well." (NOTE: The paper must be large enough for several students to work together at the same time.)

- Old magazines, catalogs, and/or newspapers

- Scissors, glue, and markers, enough for all students

- *The School Survival Guide for Kids with LD*

- **Optional:** Any book of your choice from the Children's Literature section (pages 127–142)

The Session

NOTE: You will probably need more than one session to cover all of the materials presented here. Be flexible, and be sure to allow time for students to attend one or more of the discussion groups *and* work on the group poster project.

1. Welcome the students back to the group, Ask, "Who has a 'getting organized' story they want to share?" Invite students to talk about their successes and their problems. Encourage them to keep using the handouts from sessions 18 and 19, especially "My Routine" (page 105), "Time Chart" (page 106), and "Things to Do" (page 110).

2. Say, "You all want to be successful in school, and you all want to do your best. We know that having learning differences can sometimes get in the way. During this session, we will talk about ways to be better learners and to learn in different ways. We will also talk about special tricks that can make reading, writing, spelling, and math easier for you. "

Read aloud Chapters 2 and 3 of *The School Survival Guide for Kids with LD* ("Six Ways to Be a Better Learner," pages 15–18, and "You Can Learn in Different Ways," pages 19–23). As you read the ideas in the chapters, allow time for questions and discussion.

3. Say, "Now we're going to divide up and do two different things. In one part of the room, some of you will work together on a group project. In another part of the room, some of you will join me for a small-group discussion.

"I'm going to lead three discussions: one on reading tricks, one on writing and spelling tricks, and one on math tricks. You need to pick at least one group to join. If you want to join two or all three, that's great. You'll have a chance to do the group project, too."

Show the students the large pieces of poster paper. Ask a volunteer to read the heading aloud. Say, "You can all do so many things very well. For the group project, you will cut out or draw pictures of things that you can do well, or that someone else in the group can do well. Glue each picture on the poster. Under the picture, write the name of the person it's about. If it's about more than one person, write more than one name. By the end of the project, you should all have your names under at least two or three pictures on the poster.

"You will need to work together on this project, and you will need to work quietly while the others are in the small-group discussions."

4. Announce the group you will be running first: reading, writing and spelling, or math. Give the students a chance to decide where they will go first—to the project area or the discussion group.

Let the students choose which group(s) to take part in. If necessary, encourage them to choose a group that relates to their LD.

- FOR THE READING GROUP: Read and discuss Chapter 9 of *The School Survival Guide for Kids with LD* ("Ten Ways to Be a Better Reader," pages 61–65).

- FOR THE WRITING AND SPELLING GROUP: Read and discuss Chapters 10 and 11 of *The School Survival Guide for Kids with LD* ("Ten Steps to Better Writing," pages 67–75, and "Eight Ways to Be a Better Speller," pages 77–83). Distribute the "Draw Between the Lines" and "Crossword Puzzle Form" handouts and pencils when appropriate (writing tip #7, spelling tip #3).

- FOR THE MATH GROUP: Read and discuss Chapter 12 of *The School Survival Guide for Kids with LD* ("How to Solve Your Math Problems," pages 85–103).

Allow 10–20 minutes per discussion, depending on the size of your group and the amount of time you have available.

Have each student make a verbal commitment to try at least one new learning trick. Make sure they *don't* think that they must try all of the ideas at once. That can be overwhelming. One is enough!

If at any time during the discussion you or your students come up with tricks that aren't mentioned in the *Survival Guide*, write them on the board. You may want to combine them into a new handout to give to the students at the next session.

Take a short break between groups and announce each new group before you begin it.

5. **Optional:** Read aloud from a book of your choice from the Children's Literature section. Allow time for questions and discussion.

NOTE: If some students are still working on the project after the discussion groups are over, or if some didn't get a chance to work on the project because they took part in all three discussion groups, read-aloud time is the perfect opportunity for quiet cutting and pasting.

6. End by inviting the students to share their poster(s). It's important for each student to see and read things that he or she is considered capable of doing well. It's empowering for them to know that their peers consider them to be capable. Congratulate the students on their many capabilities.

SESSION 20

Draw Between the Lines

A   B   C   D
E   F   G   H
I   J   K   L
M   N   O   P
Q   R   S   T
U   V   W   X
Y   Z

SESSION 20

Crossword Puzzle Form

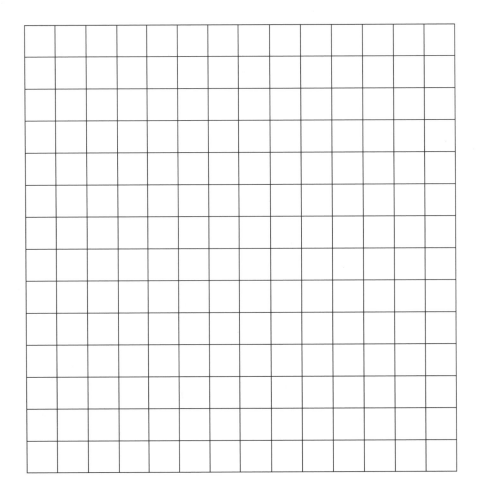

PART

5

Supplemental Sessions

Looking Toward the Future

Focus

Students identify skills they have now that show readiness for becoming an adult. They identify one or more occupations they think they would do well at and/or enjoy in the future.

Materials

Handouts

There are no handouts for this session.

Supplies

- Construction paper or tagboard (any size to make a small poster), one piece per student

- Old magazines, catalogs, and/or newspapers

- Scissors, glue, and markers, enough for all students

- *The Survival Guide for Kids with LD*

- *The School Survival Guide for Kids with LD*

- **Optional:** *The Survival Guide for Kids with LD* audio cassette

- **Optional:** Any book of your choice from the Children's Literature section (pages 127–142)

The Session

1. Welcome the students back to the group and allow a few moments for conversation. Say, "Today you will hear the stories of several people who have learning differences and have grown up to be very successful. Their stories will help you to understand that you can grow up with LD and do many important things in your life. You'll also have a chance to think about what you might want to do when you are an adult."

2. Read aloud Chapter 12 of *The Survival Guide for Kids with LD* ("What Happens When You Grow Up?," pages 71–76) or play the audio cassette. Allow time for questions and discussion.

Afterward, invite the students to describe several things they are already capable of doing that show preparation for adulthood. Ask, "Do you think that having learning differences will keep you from having certain jobs? Why or why not?" Lead the students to the awareness that they will need to apply extra effort and be extra determined because of their learning differences.

3. Read aloud Chapter 18 of *The School Survival Guide for Kids with LD* ("You Can Succeed!," pages 141–145). Allow time for questions and discussion. Ask, "What things did Alejandra have

to do to be successful?" "What about Jonathon?" "What about William?"

4. Distribute construction paper or tagboard; magazines, catalogs, and newspapers; scissors, glue, and markers. While you are handing out the materials, say, "You have probably thought about things you'd like to do when you grow up. We're going to make posters about some of those things. Print your name at the top of the paper [or board]. Then look through the magazines, catalogs, and newspapers to find at least two or three pictures that illustrate things you'd like to do or things you're good at now. Cut them out and glue them onto your poster."

Afterward, invite the students to show their posters to the group. Ask questions like, "Why did you cut out that picture?" "Why is that job one you could succeed at doing?"

5. **Optional:** Read aloud from a book of your choice from the Children's Literature section. Allow time for questions and discussion.

6. After the students have helped clean up, thank them for being willing to share their hopes and dreams for the future.

Learning from Others

Focus

Students meet an adult or an older student with LD, hear his or her story, and have the opportunity to ask questions.

Materials

Handouts

There are no handouts for this session.

Supplies

- **Optional:** Any book of your choice from the Children's Literature section (pages 127–142)

The Session

NOTE: If you can arrange to have an adult with LD come and share his or her "story" with your group, this will be an especially important and memorable session for your students. They will benefit greatly from having a "real" person with LD tell them that they can succeed at life. They are willing to hear the message of "you need to work hard, but you can make it" from someone who has been there and understands what it's like to have learning differences.

There are various ways to find a guest speaker. If there is a local chapter of the Learning Disabilities Association of America (LDA) in your area, call and ask for a recommendation. To find out if there is a local chapter in your area, call the national organization at (412) 341-1515.

If there is a local college or university that has special programs for students with LD, that may be another good source of guest speakers. Some school districts have community education offices or speakers' bureaus that may be able to help you locate a guest speaker. Some of the students in your group may have relatives with LD who are willing to come in and speak to the group.

Don't forget your own former students! One of my best group meetings happened when I invited a very successful sixth grader to talk to my fifth graders. He made more of an impact on them than any adult could have. They related better to him, and they were full of questions.

Once you find and schedule your speaker, give your students time in advance to think of and write down questions to ask the speaker. You may want to send a note home to parents, telling them about the visitor and encouraging them to help their children come up with questions.

1. Welcome the students back to the group and allow a few moments for conversation.

2. Introduce your guest. Allow time for your guest to share his or her story with the students. Afterward, have a question-and-answer session.

3. **Optional:** Read aloud from a book of your choice from the Children's Literature section. Or, if your guest feels comfortable reading aloud, invite him or her to do this. Allow time for questions and discussion.

4. End by having the students thank your guest for coming to your group.

The Road to Success

Focus

Students review what they have learned in the group and celebrate their hard work and success.

Materials

Handouts

There are no handouts specifically for this session. However, you may want to have extra copies available of handouts from previous sessions. Suggestions:

- " 'I Am, I Can' Journal" (Session 2, page 23)

- "Responding to Teasing Action Plan" (Session 8, page 50)

- "How to Send an I-Message" (Session 9, page 55)

- "Asking for Help" (Session 13, page 73)

- "Goal-Setting Steps" (Session 14, pages 78–79)

- "Ways to Help Yourself" (Session 16, pages 91–92)

- "Concentration Roadblocks and Solutions" (Session 17, page 98)

- "My Routine" (Session 18, page 105)

- "Time Chart" (Session 18, page 106)

- "Things to Do" (Session 19, page 110)

- "Organizing Your Materials" (Session 19, page 111)

Supplies

- Construction paper or tagboard (any size to make a small poster), one piece per student

- Markers, crayons, and pencils, enough for all students

- Whiteboard, chalkboard, or flip chart; marker or chalk

- A list of the general topics that were covered in the group (printed out and given to the students, written on the board, or written on a transparency and shown on the overhead)

- **Optional:** Any book of your choice from the Children's Literature section (pages 127–142)

The Session

NOTE: This session could be used as a wrap-up or final session at the end of a group or the end of a school year. It is meant to be a general review and a celebration of the students' hard work and accomplishments.

1. Welcome the students back to the group and allow a few moments for conversation.

2. Have the students review the LD awareness, coping, self-help, and study skills they worked on during the previous sessions. Use the list of general topics to assist them with remembering the activities. Encourage them to reflect on what they learned. Allow time for discussion.

3. Have the students brainstorm a list of words to describe one or more learning differences or anything else they learned about in the group. Record their words on the board.

4. Distribute construction paper or tagboard and markers, crayons, and pencils. While you are handing out the materials, say, "If someone asked you, 'What has this group taught you?,' what would you say? Think about that question. Then create a poster that shows your answer. You can use any of the words you've heard so far today, or your own words. You can use sentences or draw pictures."

Afterward, invite the students to show their posters to the group. Ask them to tell why they chose the words and pictures they did.

5. **Optional:** Read aloud from a book of your choice from the Children's Literature section. Or read a special inspirational poem you've been saving for the final session. Allow time for questions and discussion.

6. End the session—and the group—with "Students on the Road to Success" on pages 125–126. As you read the article, include as many of the students' names as possible.

7. Thank the students for their hard work and willingness to share and learn in the group. Close by saying something like this: "You make me feel so proud to have worked with you. I wish you all the best as you meet the challenges in your life, and I know that you have the courage and skills to handle them."

SESSION 23

Students on the Road to Success

Wherever we look, people are accomplishing things. Some accomplishments make the news, while others happen and almost no one hears about them.

Recently you have been working hard in this group to find out about your learning differences. Your accomplishment didn't made the front page of the newspaper, but in my opinion it should have! What you have done here is very important. You have learned about LD at an age when many people would think you couldn't understand it. You've learned to work hard and not give up. You've learned not to be afraid of making mistakes. You're realizing that your life ahead will be full of challenges, and you've learned ways to meet those challenges and succeed.

I think your accomplishment deserves a news article. In fact, I just happen to have one here, and now I'm going to read it to you.

Are you ready?

Headline: Students on the Road to Success

_____ , _____
(Your city)   (Your state)

_____
(Your local newspaper)

Recently a wonderful group of students met for _____ weeks in a very special group. They shared a common goal: working together to understand more about learning differences.

This reporter interviewed several of the group members. Their answers were interesting and very important.

Students on the Road to Success continued

When asked, "Who was helped by this group?," _____ replied, "We all were. Our parents and our friends were, too. Our LD isn't a secret anymore. We all know more about it."

_____ was asked, "When did things start to get better for the group?" He/she responded, "When we found out that we're NOT dumb and there are ways to get around our learning differences. The secret is to keep trying."

_____ was asked, "How do you feel now about your learning differences?" He/she answered, "I used to feel sorry for myself, but now I know that it's not the end of the world. It's only one part of my life."

Three of the students answered the question, "What will the future bring?" _____ said, "I know I will make mistakes along the way, but that's okay. It will help me to learn." _____ said, "I'll ask for help when I need it, try my best, and find out all the things I am good at." And _____ summed it up by saying, "I'm not going to try to hide my learning differences. If I believe in myself, I'll be able to do anything I want. I may have to work harder than some other people, but that's okay with me!"

This reporter was impressed with the students' honesty and with their understanding of their own learning differences. It's obvious that the members of this group will be happy and will do wonderful things in the future.

Session 23

Children's Literature

The Biggest Nose

Kathy Caple

(Boston, MA: Houghton Mifflin, 1985)

Themes

Feelings of inadequacy, reaction to teasing

Synopsis

Eleanor Elephant is taunted by the other animal children for having the biggest nose in the group, and she is embarrassed to find out that it is true. When Eleanor tries to shorten her nose, she learns it is fine just the way it is. Again confronted, Eleanor finds a way to stop the teasing.

Discussion Questions Based on Bloom's Taxonomy

Knowledge

- What kind of an animal was Eleanor?
- What were the animals teasing her about?
- What did she do to her nose in the bathroom?
- Name two things Eleanor's family tried to "untie" her nose.

Comprehension

- Why did Eleanor try to make her nose shorter?
- Did her idea to make her nose shorter work? Why or why not?
- Did Eleanor figure out a way to handle the other animals' teasing?

Application

- Predict what would have happened if Eleanor hadn't gotten her nose "untied."
- Tell the results of Eleanor's comments to the other animals at the end of the story.

Analysis

- How are this story and the story about Dumbo the elephant alike? How are they different?
- How does this author believe we should handle teasing?

Synthesis

- How else could Eleanor have handled her problem?

Evaluation

- What do you think of what Eleanor did to her nose?
- If you were Eleanor, would you have gotten upset with the other animals? Why or why not?
- What is the most important thing for Eleanor to do to feel better?

Do Bananas Chew Gum?

Jamie Gilson

(New York: Lothrop, Lee and Shepard Books, 1980)

Themes

Learning differences, self-esteem, coping strategies

Synopsis

Able to read and write at only a second grade level, sixth grader Sam Mott considers himself "dumb" until he is prompted to cooperate with those who think something can be done about his problem.

Discussion Questions Based on Bloom's Taxonomy

Knowledge

- What after-school job did Sam find?

- Who were the two students Sam looked through garbage with?

- What happened to the tree in Alex and Chuckie's backyard?

- What did they find in the hole?

Comprehension

- Why didn't anyone like Alicia Bliss?

- Why did Sam make jokes when he couldn't read or write something?

- Did Sam want to take the tests his parents signed their permission for? Why not?

Application

- How did Sam's difficulties affect how Alicia acted?

- Predict what would have happened if Sam's learning differences had been identified sooner.

Analysis

- How are Sam's learning differences similar to or different from your learning differences?

- What is the main idea of the story?

Synthesis

- What are some other things Sam could have done to get along better in school?

- Who, besides Alicia, did Sam help to change?

Evaluation

- If you were Sam, would you take the tests? Why or why not?

- Criticize or defend Sam's parents' actions in the story.

I'm Terrific

Marjorie Sharmat

(New York: Holiday House, 1977)

Themes

Feelings of inadequacy, self-awareness

Synopsis

Jason Bear thinks his admirable traits make him terrific and tells all of his peers so. When his self-admiration is not reinforced, Jason becomes sloppy and is nasty to his friends. Unhappy with his own behavior, Jason finally learns that happiness comes from accepting himself.

Discussion Questions Based on Bloom's Taxonomy

Knowledge

- What did Jason Bear give himself when he did something terrific?

- What did the other bears say to Jason when he told them how wonderful he was?

- What did the "new" Jason do to the other animals?

Comprehension

- Why did Jason Bear decide to act naughty?

- Why didn't Jason's mother punish him when he was naughty?

- How did Jason finally make friends with the other animals?

Application

- What else could Jason Bear have done to affirm himself, besides giving himself stars?

- Explain how the other animals and his mother's attitude changed Jason's feelings about himself.

Analysis

- What were Jason Bear's strengths?

- What were Jason Bear's weaknesses?

Synthesis

- If you were Jason Bear, would you have done anything differently?

- If you were Jason Bear's mother, how would you have helped him?

Evaluation

- Compare Jason Bear to Raymond Squirrel.

- What was wrong with Jason Bear's first plan for feeling terrific?

Josh, A Boy With Dyslexia

Caroline Janover

(Burlington, VT: Waterfront Books, 1988)

Themes

Learning differences, self-esteem, self-awareness

Synopsis

Josh Grant and his family have difficulty dealing with his learning differences. He struggles to fit in with his peers and feel an accepted part of his new school.

Discussion Questions Based on Bloom's Taxonomy

CHAPTER 1

Knowledge

- Who is Josh's brother?
- What trick did Josh play on Simon?

Comprehension

- Why did Josh's dad and Simon yell at Josh?
- How did Josh feel when he wrote the note?

Application

- What else could Josh have done instead of playing a trick on Simon?

Analysis

- Predict what will happen when Simon uses his tube of pimple medicine.

Synthesis

- What would you have done with your anger towards Simon?

Evaluation

- How do you think Josh handled his frustration? Why do you feel that way?

CHAPTER 2

Knowledge

- Who is Buck?
- Who will Josh's teacher be?

Comprehension

- Why did Josh go on a bike ride?
- How did Josh feel when he thought about the first day of school?

Application

- What else could Josh have told Buck about his learning differences?

Analysis

- Predict what will happen on the first morning of school.

Synthesis

- What would you have said to Buck about your LD?

Evaluation

- What do you think about Buck? Why?

CHAPTER 3

Knowledge

- How did Josh get to school?

Comprehension

- Why did Josh feel sick?

Application

- Predict what would have happened if Josh had walked to school.

Analysis

- How do you think Josh's mother felt as she drove away?

Synthesis

- What do you think Josh's mother will do after Josh goes to school?

Evaluation

- If you were Josh, how would you have felt in the morning?

CHAPTER 4

Knowledge

- Who did Josh meet in Mrs. Mantimer's class?

Comprehension

- What did Josh think about his old school?

Application

- Predict what would have happened if Josh had not gone to a special class.

Analysis

- How do you think Josh feels as Mrs. Mantimer is talking?

Synthesis

- How do you think Mrs. Mantimer will treat Josh?

Evaluation

- If you were Mrs. Mantimer, how would you have handled the new student?

CHAPTER 5

Knowledge

- Who did Josh meet at the kickball game?

Comprehension

- Why did Josh run the wrong way when he kicked the ball?

Application

- How did Josh's learning differences affect how he acted at the kickball game?

Analysis

- What is a weakness for Josh?

Synthesis

- If you were Simon, how would you have helped Josh at the kickball game?

Evaluation

- What should Josh have done differently at the kickball game?

CHAPTER 6

Knowledge

- Who did Josh meet in art class?

Comprehension

- Why did Kip ask Josh if dyslexia was a disease?

Application

- How did Josh's learning differences affect how he did in art class?

Analysis

- What is a strength area for Josh?

Synthesis

- If you were Josh, how would you have explained your learning differences to Kip?

Evaluation

- What should Josh have done differently when Buck teased him?

CHAPTER 7

Knowledge

- What did Josh do to Buck?
- What name did Buck call Josh?

Comprehension

- Why did Josh and Buck fight?
- Why did Josh fill his bike basket with chestnuts?

Application

- What else could Josh have done when Buck called him a "mental"?

Analysis

- Predict what will happen when Buck and Simon come home from fishing.

Synthesis

- If you were Josh, what would you have done at the game?

Evaluation

- What do you think about Josh's plan with the chestnuts?

CHAPTER 8

Knowledge

- What did Josh do before he went to bed?
- What club are Simon and Buck going to start?

Comprehension

- Why was Josh angry at dinner?
- Why was Mr. Grant angry at dinner?

Application

- What else could Mr. Grant have done when Josh wouldn't talk?

Analysis

- What is the connection between frustration and anger?

Synthesis

- If you were Josh, what would you have done at dinner?

Evaluation

- What do you think about Mr. and Mrs. Grant's actions?

CHAPTER 9

Knowledge

- What game did Josh's class play after reading?

Comprehension

- Why did Josh get angry playing the game?

Application

- Predict what would have happened if Mrs. Mantimer hadn't talked to Josh in the hall.

Analysis

- How do you think Josh felt after Mrs. Mantimer talked to him in the hall?

Synthesis

- How else could Josh have shown that he didn't want to play the game?

Evaluation

- What do you think of Josh's behavior during the game?

CHAPTER 10

Knowledge

- Where did Josh, Simon, and Buck plan to go?

Comprehension

- Why did Josh get to go fishing with Buck and Simon?

Application

- Predict what would have happened if Mrs. Grant hadn't insisted that Josh go fishing with Simon and Buck.

Analysis

- How do you think Josh felt as he overheard Simon and Buck talking?

Synthesis

- What would you have said to Buck and Simon about their fishing club?

Evaluation

- If you were Josh, would you have wanted to go fishing? Why or why not?

CHAPTER 11

Knowledge

- What happened to the boys' bikes?

Comprehension

- Why did Josh want to get help?

Application

- Predict what would have happened if the bikes hadn't been stolen.

Analysis

- What are Josh's strengths and weaknesses in a scary situation?

Synthesis

- Who (besides Simon and Buck) was Josh trying to help? Why?

Evaluation

- If you were Josh, what would you have done?

CHAPTER 12

Knowledge

- Where did Josh go on his bike?

Comprehension

- Why did Josh keep talking to himself?

Application

- Predict what would have happened if Josh had gotten in the man's car.

Analysis

- How do you think Josh felt on the bike trip home?

Synthesis

- What do you think will happen when Josh gets home?

Evaluation

- How would you have tried to get and follow directions?

CHAPTER 13

Knowledge

- Who went in the car back to the lake?

Comprehension

- How did Buck and Simon get rescued?

Application

- Predict what would have happened if Josh hadn't gotten help for Buck and Simon.

Analysis

- How do you think Josh felt when he led his dad to Simon and Buck?

Synthesis

- How else could Josh have gotten help for Simon and Buck?

Evaluation

- Do you think Josh really will be a member of the fishing club? Why or why not?

CHAPTER 14

Knowledge

- Where did Josh tell the whole story of what happened?

Comprehension

- Why did Buck ask Josh to sign his cast?

Application

- How did Josh's learning differences affect the answers he gave to the police officer?

Analysis

- How do you think Buck felt when he heard Josh's story?

Synthesis

- What would you have done to help you remember what to tell the police?

Evaluation

- Do you think Buck will be nice to Josh from now on? Why or why not?

CHAPTER 15

Knowledge

- Who called Mr. and Mrs. Grant?

Comprehension

- Why did Mrs. Mantimer call Mr. and Mrs. Grant?

Application

- Predict what would have happened if Mrs. Mantimer hadn't called Mr. and Mrs. Grant.

Analysis

- How do you think Josh felt when Mrs. Mantimer called?

Synthesis

- How else could Mr. and Mrs. Grant and Simon have learned more about Josh's learning differences?

Evaluation

- Do you think things will be different in the Grant family? If yes, how? If no, why not?

Leo the Late Bloomer

Robert Kraus

(New York: Windmill Books, 1971)

Themes

Self-esteem, patience

Synopsis

Leo, the tiger, had difficulty with everything, from talking and eating to reading and writing. Leo's father was very worried. But both he and Leo learned the meaning of the word patience.

Discussion Questions Based on Bloom's Taxonomy

Knowledge

- Name three things Leo could not do.
- Who was worried about Leo?
- What did Leo's mother say about Leo?

Comprehension

- Why was Leo's father worried?
- Why wasn't Leo's mother worried?
- What season of the year did Leo "bloom"?

Application

- Predict what would have happened if Leo's father hadn't stopped watching Leo.
- Why was spring a good time of the year for Leo to show he could do things?

Analysis

- What is the most important idea of this story?
- What is the connection between patience and success ("blooming")?

Synthesis

- What are some other things Leo's father could have done besides wait for Leo to bloom?

Evaluation

- If you were Leo's father, what would you have done?
- Do you think all children will "bloom" if we wait and watch? Why or why not?

Secrets Aren't Always for Keeps

Barbara Aiello and Jeffrey Shulman

(Frederick, MD: Twenty-First Century Books, 1988)

Themes

Learning differences, self-esteem, self-awareness

Synopsis

After successfully hiding her learning differences from her Australian pen pal, Jennifer becomes worried when her pen pal announces she is coming for a visit and she wants to spend a day at Jennifer's school.

Discussion Questions Based on Bloom's Taxonomy

Knowledge

- Who wrote Jennifer's letters?
- Where was Kay from?
- How long was Kay's visit?
- What secret did Jennifer have?
- What secret did Kay have?

Comprehension

- Why didn't Jennifer tell Kay about her learning differences?
- Why didn't Kay tell Jennifer she knew she had learning differences?

Application

- Predict what would have happened if Kay had not come for a visit.
- Explain how having a pen pal changed Jennifer's feelings about herself.

Analysis

- How do these authors believe we should handle secrets?
- How do you think Kay changed as a result of having Jennifer for a pen pal?

Synthesis

- If you were Jennifer's American friend, what could you have done differently to help her tell Kay the truth?
- How else could Jennifer have handled her problem?

Evaluation

- If you were Kay, what would you have thought about Jennifer's learning differences?
- What do you think Jennifer did correctly in her plan to tell Kay her secret?
- What do you think Jennifer did incorrectly in her plan to tell Kay her secret?

Today Was a Terrible Day

Patricia Reilly Giff

(New York: Puffin Books, 1984)

Themes

Frustration, teasing

Synopsis

Ronald's day goes from bad to worse. He accidentally squirts water on Joy, drops Miss Tyler's plant, misses the ball during recess, and is teased for his lack of reading ability.

Discussion Questions Based on Bloom's Taxonomy

Knowledge

- Who was Ronald Morgan's teacher?
- What were three things that went wrong for Ronald?
- What did Miss Tyler give Ronald at the end of the day?

Comprehension

- How did Ronald feel at the end of the day?
- Why did Miss Tyler give Ronald a note?
- Why was Ronald happy at the end of the story?

Application

- What are some other things Ronald could give Miss Tyler for her birthday?
- Predict what would have happened if Miss Tyler had not given Ronald the note.

Analysis

- Is there anything that happened to Ronald that could not really happen?
- How do you think Miss Tyler changed how she felt about Ronald as the day progressed?

Synthesis

- What else would you have done with Ronald if you were Miss Tyler?
- What could Ronald have done during the day to change what was happening?

Evaluation

- Find the errors in how Ronald handled his mistakes.
- What do you think Ronald did correctly to handle his problem?

Will the Real Gertrude Hollings Please Stand Up?

Sheila Greenwald

(Boston, MA: Little, Brown and Company, 1983)

Themes

Learning differences, self-esteem, self-awareness

Synopsis

Gertrude, an eleven-year-old girl with learning differences, spends several weeks with an overachieving cousin. They both learn a lot about themselves and the limitations labels can impose.

Discussion Questions Based on Bloom's Taxonomy

Knowledge

- Where did Gertrude's parents go for three weeks?
- Who did Gertrude stay with?
- What were "O.G.'s"?
- Who were Gertrude's two friends at school?

Comprehension

- Why didn't Albert want Gertrude to stay with them?
- How did Gertrude think she could help Albert?
- Why did Jessie work so hard to help Gertrude?

Application

- Predict what would have happened if Gertrude had not stayed with Albert.
- Explain how Gertrude's three weeks at Albert's house changed her feelings about herself.

Analysis

- How are Gertrude and Albert alike?
- What were Gertrude's strengths?
- What were Gertrude's weaknesses?

Synthesis

- Who, besides Albert, did Gertrude help change?
- If you were Gertrude's parents, would you have done anything differently?

Evaluation

- If you were Gertrude, would you have wanted to stay in her current school? Why or why not?
- What do you think Gertrude did correctly in her plan to help Albert?
- What should Gertrude have done differently in her plan with Albert?

More Children's Titles to Try

Alexander, H., *Look Inside Your Brain* (New York: Grosset & Dunlap, 1991).

DeWitt, J., *Jamie's Turn* (Milwaukee, WI: Raintree Publishers, 1984).

Dwyer, K., *What Do You Mean, I Have a Learning Disability?* (New York: Walker and Company, 1991).

Espeland, P., and Wallner, R., *Making the Most of Today: Daily Readings for Young People on Self-Awareness, Creativity, and Self-Esteem* (Minneapolis: Free Spirit Publishing Inc., 1991).

Gehret, J., *The Don't-Give-Up Kid and Learning Differences* (Fairport, NY: Verbal Images Press, 1990).

Giff, P., *The Beast in Ms. Rooney's Room* (New York: Dell-Yearling, 1984).

Kline, S., *Herbie Jones* (New York: Puffin Books, 1985).

Lasker, J., *He's My Brother* (Chicago: Albert Whitman, 1984).

Minnetonka Public Schools, *If They Can Do It, We Can Too* (Minneapolis: Deaconess Press, 1992).

Pevsner, S., *Keep Stompin' Till the Music Stops* (New York: Clarion Books, 1977).

Puckett, K., and Brown, G., *Be the Best You Can Be* (Minneapolis: Waldman House Press, 1993).

Sanford, D., *Don't Look at Me* (Hong Kong: Multnomah Press, 1986).

Sheehan, P., *Kylie's Song* (Santa Barbara, CA: Advocacy Press, 1988).

Simon, S., *Vulture: A Modern Allegory on the Art of Putting Oneself Down* (Allen, TX: Argus Communications, 1977).

Waber, B., *"You Look Ridiculous," Said the Rhinoceros to the Hippopotamus* (Boston: Houghton Mifflin, 1966).

Williams, B., *So What If I'm a Sore Loser* (New York: Harcourt Brace Jovanovich, 1981).

Recommended Reading

Borba, M., *Esteem Builders* (Rolling Hills Estates, CA: Jalmar Press, 1989).

Cuddigan, M., and Hanson, M., *Growing Pains: Helping Children Deal with Everyday Problems through Reading* (Chicago: American Library Association, 1988).

Cummings, R., and Fisher, G., *The School Survival Guide for Kids with LD (Learning Differences)* (Minneapolis: Free Spirit Publishing Inc., 1991).

Fisher, G., and Cummings, R., *The Survival Guide for Kids with LD (Learning Differences)* (Minneapolis: Free Spirit Publishing Inc., 1990).

Fox, C., and Malian, I.M., *Social Acceptance: Key to Mainstreaming* (Rolling Estates, CA: B.L. Winch, 1983).

Mayo, P., and Waldo, P., *Scripting: Social Communications for Adolescents* (Eau Claire, WI: Thinking Publications, 1986).

McGinnis, E., and Goldstein, A., *Skillstreaming the Elementary School Child* (Champaign, IL: Research Press, 1984).

Index

About the Author

Susan McMurchie received her B.A. from Gustavus Adolphus College in St. Peter, Minnesota; her L.D. certification from the University of St. Thomas in St. Paul, Minnesota; and her M.A. from St. Mary's College in Winona, Minnesota. She has taught third grade and is currently teaching students with learning differences in the Rosemount/Apple Valley/Eagan school district in Minnesota.

Susan is active in her church and in the Apple Valley Fire Department Auxiliary. She has served as secretary of Dakota County United Educators. She is also on the board of the LDM 196 chapter of Learning Disabilities of America. In 1992, Susan received the Learning Disabilities of Minnesota Professional Excellence Award.

Susan lives in Apple Valley, Minnesota, with her husband, Tom, and her daughter, Ryan.

MORE FREE SPIRIT BOOKS

The Survival Guide for Kids with LD*
*(Learning Differences)
by Gary Fisher, Ph.D. and Rhoda Cummings, Ed.D.
Solid information and sound advice for children labeled "learning disabled." Explains LD in terms kids can understand, defines different kinds of LD, discusses LD programs, and emphasizes that kids with LD can be winners, too. Ages 8–12; reading level 2.7 (grade 2, 7th month).
$8.95; 104 pp.; illus.; s/c; 6" x 9"

Also available:
The Survival Guide for Kids with LD Audio Cassette
96 minutes on 1 cassette
Cassette only: $10.00
Book with cassette: $16.95

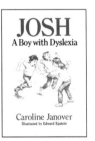

Josh
A Boy with Dyslexia
by Caroline Janover
This gripping story about a 5th-grade boy who is dyslexic explores the mind and heart of child with LD and helps the reader better understand learning differences. Includes questions and answers about dyslexia and LD.
Ages 8–12.
Softcover: $7.95; 100 pp.; illus.; 5 1/2" x 8"
Hardcover: $11.95; 100 pp.; illus.; 5 1/2" x 8"

Making the Most of Today
Daily Readings for Young People on Self-Awareness, Creativity, and Self-Esteem
by Pamela Espeland and Rosemary Wallner
Quotes from Eeyore, Mariah Carey, Dr. Martin Luther King, Jr., and others guide young people through a year of positive thinking, problem-solving, and practical lifeskills. Ages 11 and up.
$8.95; 392 pp.; s/c; 4" x 7"

The School Survival Guide for Kids with LD
Ways to Make Learning Easier and More Fun
by Rhoda Cummings, Ed.D. and Gary Fisher, Ph.D.
Kids learn how to organize their time, set goals, and stick up for themselves. "School tools" build confidence in reading, writing, spelling, math, and more. Special chapters tell how to handle conflict, stay out of trouble, cope with testing, and get help from adults. Ages 8 and up; reading level 2.7 (grade 2, 7th month).
$10.95; 176 pp.; illus.; s/c; 6" x 9"

The Survival Guide for Teenagers with LD*
*(Learning Differences)
by Rhoda Cummings, Ed.D., and Gary Fisher, Ph.D.
Advice, information, and resources to help teenagers with LD succeed at school and prepare for life as adults. Ages 13 and up; reading level 6.2 (grade 6, 2nd month).
$11.95; 200 pp.; illus.; s/c; 6" x 9"

Also available:
The Survival Guide for Teenagers with LD Audio Cassettes
226 minutes on 2 cassettes
Cassettes only: $19.95
Book with cassettes: $28.90

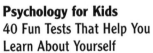

Psychology for Kids
40 Fun Tests That Help You Learn About Yourself
by Jonni Kincher
Based on sound psychological concepts, this fascinating book promotes self-discovery, self-awareness, and self-esteem. It helps young people answer questions like, "Are you an introvert or an extrovert?" and "What body language do you speak?" and empowers them to make good choices about their lives.
Ages 10 and up.
$11.95; 160 pp.; illus.; s/c; 11" x 8 1/2"

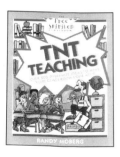